COCKTAILS
BY FLAVOR

Salvatore Calabrese

COCKTAILS
BY FLAVOR

MORE THAN **390**

RECIPES to TEMPT the TASTE BUDS

STERLING EPICURE
New York

To my dear wife, Sue, and my family: thanks again for your support.

STERLING EPICURE
New York

An Imprint of Sterling Publishing
387 Park Avenue South
New York, NY 10016

Design by Christine Heun

ISBN 978-1-4027-8627-3

Distributed in Canada by Sterling Publishing
c/o Canadian Manda Group, 165 Dufferin Street
Toronto, Ontario, Canada M6K 3H6
Distributed in the United Kingdom by GMC Distribution Services
Castle Place, 166 High Street, Lewes, East Sussex, England BN7 1XU
Distributed in Australia by Capricorn Link (Australia) Pty. Ltd.
P.O. Box 704, Windsor, NSW 2756, Australia

For information about custom editions, special sales, and premium and corporate purchases,
please contact Sterling Special Sales at 800-805-5489 or specialsales@sterlingpublishing.com.

Manufactured in China

2 4 6 8 10 9 7 5 3 1

www.sterlingpublishing.com

contents

introduction

O n Italy's Amalfi Coast there is one flavor above all others that hangs in the air day and night: the flavor of lemon. This is because the daredevil drive along the coast to my hometown of Maiori is where the world-famous limoncello liqueur is produced. Lemon groves line the roads, set on tiers of ledges that cascade down the mountainside. Tree branches are laden with lemons, their skins ripening from pale to dark in the warmth of a Mediterranean sun.

From childhood to adulthood, a sense of flavor filled my life. So when my publisher suggested writing a book on cocktails by flavor, I was immediately taken back to those citrus-flavored early years.

I learned about flavor from Raffaello, the bartender who taught me nearly everything I knew about the bar business back then. In our quiet moments, he would mix a cocktail, ask me to blind-taste it, then tell him the flavors that were in it. We would do this time and time again as I learned how to detect the bitter taste of Campari, a light Scotch whisky, brandy in a Sidecar, and the Brandy Alexander with its creamy finish. I grew up with the classics, which remain among my favorite cocktails to this day.

Sip by sip I savored the flavors that filled my mouth, setting off sensory connections that had lain dormant until the very second that the aged rum or fine Scotch malt whisky whacked against my taste buds. "Wow!" and "Wow!" again echoed in my mind as my taste memory worked overtime to file away these sensations.

Throughout my career, there has been a certainty: one flavor is not more popular than another. Yes, flavors come and go with trends because drinkers like to follow the fashion and like to drink what's *in* right now. Classicists rarely stray from the tried and true that they look forward to, such as a Martini or a Manhattan, because the taste of a cocktail is why you drink it. You do not usually choose a cocktail because of its fancy name or the incredibly cool, stylish glass in which it is served.

For decades, the number one spirit of choice has been vodka, straight and pure and, ironically, tasteless. However, this lack of flavor has made it perfect as a spirit base. You can combine anything with it. Gin has always had a unique flavor, due to the combinations of botanicals in it. But vodka is the preferable base for building upon. Take the Cosmopolitan—would cranberry and lime juices and Cointreau taste the same with rum? No.

These days, vodka distillers manufacture ranges of triple- and quadruple-distilled, and triple-filtered, vodkas to convince drinkers that vodka can have a true spirit flavor. And vodkas are also produced in a wide range of intoxicating flavors, including cherry, vanilla, rose, pepper, raspberry, peach, grapefruit, black currant, mandarin, mango, orange, horseradish, lemon, and pear.

Rum has been flavored with coconut for some decades, and now tequila producers are flavoring a few of their exquisite tequilas. Exotic liqueurs now join the familiar sweet liqueurs and cordials on the shelf to add another taste level. Juice manufacturers explore new flavors such as pomegranate and juice from the açaí berry, which leads me to the other factor in this current explosion of flavors. A sense of "How healthy is what I'm putting into my body?" reigns. People want the thrill of alcohol but they are also health-conscious.

It is a stirring time to be a bartender. The trend toward infusions offers a wealth of flavors that can be made following the age-old, do-it-yourself tradition of merging spirit and flavor. Herbs such as lavender and rosemary, spices such as chiles and saffron, and vegetables such as cucumber offer opportunities for cocktail recipes.

This book is divided into three sections. The first is called "Getting It Right" and contains the basics of bar equipment, glassware, preparing a cocktail, how to store spirits and wine, how to make a garnish, advice on ice, a list of terms you will come across in the recipes, and spirit measurements.

The second section is called "True Spirits" and examines the flavors of brandy, gin, rum, tequila, vodka, Scotch, whiskey, and sake. The third section is an "A to Z of Flavors," within which recipes are presented under bitters, fruits, herbs and flowers, nut flavors, spices, sweet and creamy, unusual flavors, vegetables, and wine flavors.

Finally, experimenting with flavors is essential to the development of a successful cocktail list. For me, however, no other flavor surpasses that of a cocktail glass filled with gin straight from the freezer, a whiff of vermouth, and the teardrops of a twist of lemon. My Martini!

—Salvatore Calabrese

GETTING IT
RIGHT

flavor

Now there's a word to start the taste buds watering. Strictly defined, the word *flavor* is about the blend of taste and smell sensations evoked by a substance in the mouth. Every bartender will agree with that definition. Each cocktail he or she makes is a blend of aromatic sensations, with every sip a palate pleaser.

Here's the science . . . for those who like things proven. Recent research has confirmed that bitter, sweet, salty, and sharp (sour) are the only tastes that humans can detect. Taste buds, little organs located all over the tongue, interpret or pick up the sense of which flavors are in food and drink. All other flavors are experienced primarily through aroma with the exception of the fiery heat of chile pepper, which is a chemically induced sensation on the palate. Also, it's been confirmed that an affinity for sweet and an aversion to bitter flavors are part of our genetic makeup.

There are many combinations of tastes, such as sweet/sour, bitter/salty, sour/salty, bitter/sweet, sweet/sour/spicy, sour/spicy, bitter/sour, etc. Adding the spicy sensation as well as aroma to this taste lineup results in the layers of flavor present in every good cocktail.

Development of your palate is the key to discovering one flavor among all others. By refining your palate, you learn which flavors you like and dislike and build up a "flavor memory bank." I recommend you move one ingredient at a time all over your mouth so

SAMPLE COCKTAILS BY CATEGORY

SWEET

Banana Daiquiri (page 64)

Grasshopper (page 160)

Golden Cadillac (page 160)

SHARP (SOUR)

Whiskey Sour (page 85)

Margarita (page 86)

Lemon Drop (page 84)

BITTER

Campari Nobile (page 52)

Negroni (page 55)

Apothecary Cocktail (page 55)

SALTY

Dirty Martini (page 94)

Salty Dog (page 78)

Classic Tequila Shot (page 41)

SPICY

Cinnamon May (page 150)

Ginger Nut (page 151)

Saffron Love (page 153)

you can register its flavor. Then you can "search" for it when it is layered with others.

Basically, a cocktail consists of a spirit base, a modifier (aromatizer), and a coloring agent or special flavoring. In exotic cocktails there may be more than one flavoring agent, and some recipes have club soda, ginger ale, or sparkling water for a special effervescent effect.

Modifiers are the calming elements and include vermouth, wine, fruit juice, cream, eggs, and sugar.

The coloring agent or special flavoring category includes fruit syrups such as grenadine or orgeat, and other liqueurs and cordials. It is important that the additions do not overwhelm the flavor of the base spirit but allow it to come through in the finished cocktail.

Some cocktail flavors are simple and true, such as strawberry, while others can be a combination of several fruits, vegetables, herbs, and spirits, which together create a new and distinct flavor.

When you look at a recipe with several types of fruit juice in it, you may wonder why the recipe is placed in a particular category. Each cocktail has been placed in the category of the last, lingering flavor that dominates the finish. In a Mai Tai, for instance, it is the flavor of the orgeat that lingers in the mouth. In a Dirty Martini, it is the olive flavor that remains, with the strength of the vodka.

The section that begins on page 29 presents cocktails dominated by true spirit flavors—brandy, gin, rum, tequila, vodka, whiskey, and sake (which is more a rice wine than a spirit, but I have included it here).

In the various sections, you might be surprised to discover some new and exotic flavors that offer an unusual experience for your palate, such as lush pomegranate juice, full of antioxidants, or a horseradish-flavored vodka, and a recipe using açaí berry juice. There is even a category of cocktails made with beet juice! The "A to Z of Flavors" section begins with bitters, fruits, herbs, nut flavors, spices, sweet and creamy, unusual flavors, and vegetables and ends with a selection of wine-flavored cocktails, including Champagne.

A piece of advice: Measure the ingredients to the last drop, and your cocktail will turn out fine. Enjoy!

bartender's tools

Certain tools and equipment can help you make delicious cocktails. Following is a list of my favorites. The items on this list are readily available at most kitchen supply stores.

BAR KNIFE
A small, sharp knife used for slicing fruit.

BAR SPOON
A long, straight-handled spoon with a small bowl at the end.

BLENDER
Use to combine spirits, juice, heavy cream, fruit, and ice.

BOTTLE OPENER
Choose a strong opener that feels good in your hand.

CHAMPAGNE STOPPER
Useful for keeping the bubbles in a bottle.

CHOPPING BOARD
Use to slice fruit for garnishes.

COCKTAIL STICKS
Use for spearing pieces of fruit and cherries for garnishes.

CORKSCREW
Use to open wine bottles.

DASH BOTTLE AND DASH POURER
Use for drops and dashes of bitters.

ICE BUCKET AND TONGS
Essential for making chilled drinks. Use the tongs to lift the cubes.

ICE SCOOP
Use to add ice to a shaker or blender.

JUICER
Important for making fresh citrus juice.

MINI GRATER
Use to dust a drink with chocolate or nutmeg.

MIXING GLASS
Use to mix two or more ingredients with a bar spoon.

MUDDLER
Use to mash sprigs of mint or fruit into a pulp in the bottom of a mixing glass, shaker, or old-fashioned glass.

JIGGER, OR PONY JIGGER
Use for correct measures to balance the flavor and strength of a cocktail. (For types, see page 26.)

SALT AND PEPPER GRINDERS
Use to provide a spicy flavor in cocktails such as the Bloody Mary.

SHAKER
Use to combine various spirits and juice together with ice. (For types, see page 10.)

SPIRITS POURER
Fits onto spirits bottles to improve control and prevent spillage.

STIRRERS
Stirrers can be made of glass or silver.

STRAINER
Use with a shaker to pour just the liquid into a glass.

STRAWBERRY HULLER
Use to remove the stem and hull from a strawberry.

STRAWS
Use short straws for small glasses; for highballs and goblets, use two longer straws. Plain straws are best.

ZESTER
Use on citrus peels to make garnishes.

Boston shaker

regular shaker

mixing glass,
bar spoon,
strainer

muddler

bitters bottle

small bottle

pony jigger

Champagne
stopper

tongs

corkscrew

spirits
pourer

selecting your glassware

In my experience, fine, clear glasses reveal a cocktail in all its beauty. Traditionally, each type of drink has a glass shape specifically for it. For instance, a long drink needs a highball, a Martini is served in a Martini/cocktail glass, a margarita is at home in a Champagne coupe, and an Old Fashioned belongs in its namesake.

When buying stemmed glasses, seek out those with a design on the stem. It adds a visual interest to the presentation. Avoid any type of glass with a colored bowl. This hides the color of a cocktail.

Always handle a stemmed glass by the stem, not the bowl. This helps keep the cocktail chilled. And keep a clean dish towel nearby to polish glasses and to remove any traces of detergent.

MAIN GLASS TYPES AND SIZES

Cocktail . . . . .4 to 12 oz (12 to 36 cl)
Old-fashioned . . . . .6 to 8 oz (18 to 24 cl)
Double old-fashioned . . . . .10 to 12 oz (30 to 36 cl)
Shot . . . . .1½ oz (4.5 cl)
Liqueur or cordial glass . . . . 2 to 3 oz (6 to 9 cl)
Highball .10 to 12 oz (30 to 36 cl)
White wine . . . . 8 to 12 oz (24 to 36 cl)
Red wine . . . . 9 to 14 oz (27 to 42 cl)

There are many glass styles. However, you need only a basic selection of four. The cocktail glass is by far the most popular shape for almost any cocktail served without ice. A flute is essential for Champagne cocktails, and an old-fashioned glass is good for short drinks. The highball is king of the long-drink glasses.

Champagne Coupe

 Traditionally used for Champagne, it is now popular for serving some of the classic cocktails.

Champagne Flute

 The flute shape brings the bubbles to the surface.

Cocktail

 A 4-oz cocktail glass is best for these recipes.

Cognac

 The balloon-shaped glass for Cognac.

Goblet

 This is best for exotic cocktails with lots of color and a few juices.

Highball

 Used for long drinks. Also known as a tumbler.

Hot Toddy/Irish Coffee

 Designed to withstand the heat of coffee.

Liqueur

 A small glass used for serving after-dinner digestifs.

Old-fashioned

 A short glass with a heavy base that sits nicely in the palm of your hand.

Piña Colada

 The glass style for the famous Piña Colada cocktail.

Shot

 Designed for a measure of a strong spirit that is downed in one gulp.

White and Red Wine

 Wine glasses are good for cocktails that include mixers, juices, and fancy garnishes.

storing spirits & wine

storing & serving champagne

Champagne and sparkling wine should ideally be kept on a rack in a horizontal position. Try to maintain a consistent cool temperature. A warning: Do not freeze a Champagne bottle to chill it quickly. This can ruin the contents. Always use clean Champagne flutes that have been wiped clean of any traces of dishwashing detergent residue.

opening champagne

Wrap a clean towel around the neck of the bottle and hold it firmly in one hand. With the other, remove the wire cage from the cork. Place your hand over the cork and slowly twist it to *gently* ease it from the bottle.

When pouring Champagne and sparkling wine, aim for the middle of the flute and pour slowly. Pause after a few moments to let the bubbles subside, then start pouring again. Fill to only three-quarters full.

storing wine

Store red wine at cool room temperature, not in the refrigerator. It is best to store bottles on their side to keep the cork wet.

White wines are best kept chilled on their side in the refrigerator. It is best not to chill bottles in the freezer.

storing spirits & eaux-de-vie in the freezer

When you place a bottle of spirit such as gin, vodka, aquavit, Poire William, kirsch, framboise, or Kümmel in the freezer, you will discover that it does not freeze. This is because the spirit is 80 proof (40 percent alcohol by volume). Be careful not to put a bottle containing a spirit with alcohol by volume lower than that, say, 74 proof (37 percent alcohol), in the freezer because the spirit will freeze and the bottle may even crack. Storing spirits in the freezer helps ensure truly cold drinks.

chilling a cocktail glass

Rule number one: Always chill a cocktail glass before you pour any liquid into it. The frosted effect makes a drink look fabulous and appealing.

Put the required number of glasses in the freezer for a few hours before you need to use them. Or fill them with crushed ice—this will chill the glass before the cocktail is poured in. Discard this ice before adding the drink.

preparing cocktails

using a shaker

A recipe that contains spirits, juice, and/or light cream can be shaken. The two most common shakers are the Boston shaker and the regular metal shaker.

The Boston shaker has two pieces— one is metal; the other is clear glass. The ingredients are poured into the glass so you can see what you are doing, then ice is added. The metal part covers the glass, and is sealed with a gentle slap of the palm.

Turn the shaker upside down and shake. After the drink is shaken, the ingredients should end up in the metal part. Let the drink settle for a moment before parting the two sections. If you can't open the shaker easily, place your thumb under the center section, where the metal and glass meet, and push gently. This will break the air vacuum inside.

To serve the drink, pour it through a bar strainer placed firmly over the shaker's opening.

The regular shaker consists of a base, a top with a built-in strainer, and a lid. It's usually compact and easy to handle. Always be sure you hold the lid down firmly when you shake. If it gets stuck, ease the lid up with both thumbs. Sometimes a quick, hard twist will do the trick.

Also, if you have shaken it for a while, wipe down the outside with a cloth. This warms the sides and loosens the vacuum.

how to muddle

To muddle, you need a muddler. Sometimes, the end of a bar spoon has a muddler attached. More bartenders are using this method nowadays; instead of bashing fruit to a pulp, as when using a blender, muddling brings out the essence without bitterness, and the freshness of the fruit remains intact.

Fruit or mint is generally muddled directly in the base of the serving glass or in a shaker. Choose a glass with a heavy base. Dice the fruit and place it in the glass or shaker. Add sugar and/or a dash of spirit or wine (if the recipe calls for either or both) and push down on the fruit until the juice oozes out.

This photograph was taken after one minute of muddling diced limes. You can see how much juice can be released through constant pressure. ❯ ❯ ❯

using a mixing glass

Cocktails whose ingredients mix easily and must be served chilled are made (built) directly in a mixing glass, then poured into a glass. Always place about six ice cubes into the mixing glass first and, using a bar spoon, stir the ice around to chill the glass. Using a bar strainer, strain off any excess water. Add each spirit and stir the mixture well. Strain the drink into the glass.

Classic cocktails, such as the Manhattan, are always stirred in a mixing glass.

2 Place the bar spoon well under the ice cubes and stir to combine the spirits.

1 Note how much ice has been put in the mixing glass and how the spirit passes over the ice cubes. It gets chilled on the way.

3 Pour slowly from a height, being careful not to splash over the edge of the glass.

creating a layered drink

The answer to layering drinks such as the Slipslider (page 65) is in the density of each spirit in the recipe. Generally, layered drinks are made in shot or liqueur glasses. All you need are a steady hand and a bar spoon.

To determine the order of ingredients (unless it's specified in the recipe), look for the alcohol percentage on each label—the lower it is, the more sugar the ingredient contains and the more dense it is, like a syrup. The ingredient lowest in alcohol is your first layer, and so on.

To pour the second, less-heavy ingredient, pick up the bar spoon and place it in the glass on the edge of the first layer, with the back of the spoon facing up. Pour the second ingredient slowly onto the highest point of the spoon, so the liquid gradually flows downward to create a distinct layer. Repeat for each of the successively lighter layers. The bar spoon method can be used for any recipe that directs you to "float" an ingredient over a drink.

blending cocktails

As a general rule, blend any recipe that contains heavy cream, solid ingredients, and ice that needs to be broken down. How much to make? Usually a recipe is for one drink, but with a blender it is sometimes best to make two or more drinks at one time, especially if you are making the cocktails during a party.

Always wash, peel, and dice fruit before adding it to the blender. And make sure there is enough liquid in the blender to allow ingredients to liquefy.

Some blended recipes require the mixture to be strained through a sieve, making a liquid with a finer texture. This is easy to do: Place the sieve over the glass and pour small amounts of the mixture into the sieve. With a teaspoon or bar spoon, mash the mixture until most of the liquid has passed through the holes in the wire mesh. Then discard the remaining pits or flesh and pour in an additional small amount, repeating the process.

Blended cocktails are best served immediately, so they don't melt. You can blend the fruit and spirits before an event and place the mixture in the refrigerator, but do not add creamy ingredients or ice until the last minute.

garnishes

Garnishes are the finishing touch. First, consider the flavor of the cocktail you are making. Match the garnish with the dominant flavor. Second, consider the color of the garnish. Select something that will look as if it belongs to the drink. Third, a garnish must be in proportion to the size of the glass and not look like an afterthought.

Note that when a recipe calls for a wedge or slice of lemon, orange, or lime and an old-fashioned glass or highball, the garnish always goes in the drink.

Some garnishes, such as strawberries, can be dropped into a drink or perched on the rim. To make a strawberry fan, remove the green stem and leaves, if desired, and slice the berry thinly, starting at the tip, without cutting all the way through. Fan out the slices and slip the berry onto the rim of the glass. Or use a whole hulled strawberry by making a small slit in the bottom and slipping it over the rim. See page 15 to make an apple fan.

frost/crust the rim of a glass

Some cocktails, such as a classic margarita, require a frosted (or crusted) rim, which adds flavor and texture as well as an attractive appearance to a drink.

To frost a rim, pour some fine sea salt or superfine (caster) sugar into a saucer, as indicated in the drink recipe. Rub the rim with a wedge of lemon, orange, or lime (according to the recipe), and dip the rim in the salt or sugar.

① Cut a slit in the wedge of lemon and insert the wedge over the rim of the cocktail glass.

② Make sure the sugar (or salt) is on both sides of the rim and that there is enough of the substance to remain on the glass when you shake it.

make an apple fan

Cut off one side of a small green apple, avoiding the core. Using a sharp knife, cut the piece into thin vertical slices. Take five of these in your hand and fan them out like a pack of cards. Pierce the base of the fan with a toothpick.

make a slice

Wash and dry a lime and place it on the cutting board. Hold it firmly with the tip of your fingers. With a knife, slice firmly through the skin and flesh to make a slender slice. Use the slices cut from the middle of the lime.

make a wedge

Cut a fresh lime in half vertically. Place it flesh down on the cutting board. With a knife, cut at an angle into the lower edge of the lime to slice a wedge that is wider at the peel and tapers to an edge. Repeat as needed.

make a twist

A twist of lemon, lime, or orange is the type of garnish you will use for many of the classic cocktails, as well as some of the newer-style Martinis.

The secret of the twist is in its ability to add the fruit's essence to a cocktail without drowning the other flavors in the drink. A hint is more interesting than a wallop! When twisting the peel, you can see the drops of essence that fall into the drink. It is also a way to add flair to your method of making a drink. A stylish finishing touch is always welcome.

You will see a bartender squeeze a twist of lemon into a gin or vodka Martini, a classic Rusty Nail, and the Sazerac. In many cases, the bartender will twist and then drop the peel into the glass.

The twist has a second role to play in the making of a cocktail. Sometimes a bartender will add a little hint of flavor by wiping the twist around the rim of the glass. When you pick up the glass, the aroma of the fruit is right under your nose.

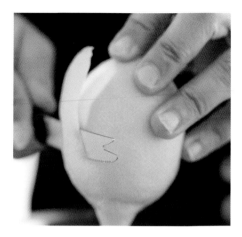

① Hold the fruit upright. With a sharp knife, cut a reasonably wide section from the side of a fresh, clean lemon, orange, or lime.

② Place the section on the cutting board and trim each side neatly.

③ Turn the piece of rind over, and gently cut off the white pith. Discard the pith.

④ Hold the twist over the drink with your fingertips and squeeze it to release the teardrops of essence.

⑤ You can also run the twist around the rim of the glass, using the pith side, to add citrus oil to the rim. This is a quick movement right around, and then you can drop the twist into the cocktail.

useful information

flavored spirits

In recent years, we have seen an influx of flavored spirits, and bartenders love to experiment in producing their own infusions with ever more unusual flavors. This is not a new idea, but one that began with the early production of vodka when honey, herbs, and flower essences were used to mask the harshness of these early spirits. In the West Indies, rums were flavored and colored with spices and burnt sugar. Even the Romans, 2,000 years ago, used herbs and spices to flavor their wine to mask the acidity and make the wine more palatable.

how to make a syrup

Many recipes in this book call for simple syrup or flavored syrups. Most of these syrups can be found in many supermarkets and online, but you can make your own by following these easy recipes.

Simple Syrup

2 cups	sugar
1 cup	water

Combine the sugar and water in a small saucepan and heat over medium heat, stirring occasionally, until the sugar is dissolved and the syrup thickens. Remove from the heat, let cool, and bottle.

Chamomile Syrup

2 cups	water
1 cup	dried chamomile flowers
2 cups	sugar

Bring the water to a boil in a small saucepan. Add the chamomile flowers, reduce the heat to low, and simmer gently for a few minutes. Remove from the heat and let the mixture sit for 15 minutes to allow the flavors to develop. Strain through a fine mesh sieve into a clean saucepan. Add the sugar and heat over medium heat, stirring, until the sugar is dissolved and the syrup has thickened. Remove from the heat, let cool, and bottle.

Cinnamon Syrup

2 cups	water
4	cinnamon sticks
1½ cups	sugar

Combine water and cinnamon sticks in a small saucepan and bring to a boil. Reduce the heat to low and simmer 10 minutes, stirring occasionally. Strain through a fine mesh sieve into a bowl. Return the cinnamon water to the saucepan and bring to a boil. Add the sugar and stir until it is dissolved and the syrup has thickened. Remove from the heat, let cool, and bottle.

Coconut Syrup

2 cups	sugar
1 cup	water
1 cup	grated coconut
2 tsps	coconut extract

Combine the sugar and water in a small saucepan and heat the mixture over medium heat, stirring occasionally, until the sugar is dissolved and the syrup has thickened slightly. Remove from the heat and stir in the grated coconut and coconut extract. Once the syrup is cool, let it stand for about 2 hours more to allow the flavors to develop, then strain and bottle.

Ginger Syrup

2 cups	sugar
1 cup	water
1/2 cup	fresh grated ginger

Combine the sugar and water in a small saucepan and heat the mixture over medium heat, stirring occasionally, until the sugar is dissolved. Reduce the heat to low and simmer, stirring occasionally, until it begins to thicken. Stir in the ginger and continue to simmer gently, stirring occasionally, for another 10 minutes. Remove from the heat and let cool. Strain through a fine mesh sieve, then bottle.

Gooseberry Syrup

2 cups	sugar
1 cup	water
1 cup	fresh gooseberries

Combine the sugar, water and gooseberries in a small saucepan and heat the mixture over a medium heat, stirring occasionally, until the sugar is dissolved. Reduce the heat to low and simmer about 10-15 minutes. Remove from the heat and let cool. Pour through a fine mesh sieve to remove the berry solids, then bottle.

Grenadine Syrup

2 cups	sugar
1 cup	water
1 cup	fresh pomegranate juice

Combine the sugar and water in a small saucepan and heat the mixture over medium heat, stirring occasionally, until the sugar is dissolved. Reduce the heat to low and simmer the mixture until it begins to thicken, then stir in the pomegranate juice. Remove from the heat and let cool. Strain through a fine mesh sieve, then bottle.

Herb-Flavored Syrup

2 cups	water
small bunch	herb of choice
	(sage, thyme, basil,
	rosemary, lemongrass,
	lavender, etc.)
2 cups	sugar

Combine the water and herbs in a small saucepan and bring to a boil. Reduce the heat to low and simmer until the water is reduced by half, 10–15 minutes. Remove from the heat. When the herb water is cool, taste the mixture. If it is not strong enough, add more herbs, stir, and let stand for a few more minutes. Strain the liquid through a fine mesh sieve into a bowl. Return the herb water to the saucepan, add the sugar, and heat gently until the sugar is dissolved and the syrup has thickened. Let cool, bottle, and store in the refrigerator.

Honey Syrup

2 cups	set (creamed) honey
	(preferably clover honey)
1 cup	water

Combine the honey and water in a small saucepan and heat the mixture over medium heat, stirring occasionally, until the honey is dissolved. Let cool and bottle.

Mango Syrup

2 cups	sugar
1 cup	water
1 cup	mango puree

Combine the sugar and water in a small saucepan and heat the mixture over medium heat, stirring occasionally, until the sugar is dissolved. Reduce the heat to low and simmer, stirring occasionally, until it begins to thicken. Stir in the mango puree and continue to simmer gently, stirring occasionally, for another 10 minutes. Remove from the heat and let cool. Strain through a fine mesh sieve, then bottle.

Passion Fruit Syrup

2 cups	sugar
1 cup	water
8	fresh passion fruits
	(seeds only)

Combine the sugar and water in a small saucepan and heat over medium heat, stirring occasionally, until the sugar is dissolved. Add the passion fruit seeds from 6 of the passion fruits and simmer for a couple of minutes. Remove from the heat, add the remaining seeds from the other fruits, and let cool. (The addition of fruit seeds that are not boiled adds some extra freshness to the syrup, while the boiled fruit seeds impart a deeper flavor.) Once the syrup is cool, let it stand for about 2 hours more to allow the flavors to develop. Strain through a fine mesh sieve, then bottle.

Pineapple Syrup

1 cup	pineapple chunks
2 cups	sugar
1 cup	water

Puree the pineapple in a blender. Combine the sugar and water in a small saucepan and heat the mixture over medium heat, stirring, until the sugar is dissolved and the syrup has thickened. Stir in the pineapple puree, reduce the heat to low, and simmer gently for 10 minutes. Remove from the heat and let cool. Strain through a fine mesh sieve, then bottle.

Raspberry Syrup

2 cups	sugar
1 cup	water
1 cup	fresh raspberries

Combine the sugar, water, and raspberries in a small saucepan and heat over medium heat, stirring occasionally, until the sugar is dissolved. Reduce the heat to low and simmer about 10–15 minutes. Remove from the heat and let cool. Pour through a fine mesh sieve to remove the berry solids, then bottle.

Rose Syrup

3	roses
2 cups	sugar
1 cup	water

Wash and dry the rose petals. Combine the sugar and water in a small saucepan and heat the mixture over medium heat, stirring occasionally, until the sugar is dissolved. Reduce the heat to low, add the rose petals, and simmer very gently for 15 minutes, stirring occasionally (do not boil). Remove from the heat and let cool 2–3 hours to allowing the flavors to develop. Strain through a fine mesh sieve, then bottle.

Saffron Syrup

2 cups	sugar
1 cup	water
2 or 3	strands of saffron

Combine the sugar and water in a small saucepan and heat the mixture over medium heat, stirring occasionally, until the sugar is dissolved. Reduce the heat to low and simmer, stirring occasionally, until it begins to thicken. Stir in the saffron. Remove from the heat and let cool. Strain through a fine mesh sieve, then bottle.

Vanilla Syrup

2 cups	sugar
1 cup	water
1	vanilla bean, split lengthwise
1 tsp	vanilla extract

Combine the sugar and water in a small saucepan. Scrape the seeds from the vanilla bean into the pan and add the pod. Heat the mixture over medium heat, stirring occasionally, until the sugar is dissolved. Reduce the heat to low and simmer about 10–15 minutes. Remove from the heat, discard the pod, and stir in the vanilla extract. Let cool, strain, and bottle.

a note about egg white

Combining egg white with other ingredients and then shaking gives a drink a white frothy head. If, for health reasons, you are concerned about using fresh egg white, use pasteurized egg white instead.

juicing limes

When choosing a lime, the freshest one will have a paler green skin. If its rind is dark green, you will get less juice from it. Some bartenders roll a lime prior to juicing. The rolling action separates the juice from the pith inside the lime. You can also put the lime in hot water for about 30 seconds. This action releases the juice inside. Then cut the skin with a sharp fruit knife.

Just squeezing the fruit is not enough to get the juice out. Use a hand juicer—it also stops the seeds (if there are any) from escaping into the drink.

ice

Ice must be fresh and dry. Use filtered or bottled water to make ice. Ice should taste only of water. Ice may be crushed, shaved, cracked, or cubed. Cracked and shaved ice melt faster than ice cubes; when these smaller pieces are added to a drink, the spirit is more immediately diluted. With solid ice cubes, the ice holds its water for a longer period while the drink is sipped. The average ice cube contains between 1 and $1\frac{1}{2}$ oz (3 and 4.5 cl) water, but the ice melts very slowly.

As a general rule, ice cubes are used for cocktails made in a shaker. Crushed ice is used for drinks created in a blender, not in a glass, unless the recipe specifically states, "Use crushed ice." Ice cubes are used in old-fashioned glasses and highballs, but never in a cocktail glass, except to chill the glass before pouring in the drink.

Remember, do not use the ice remaining in a shaker for the next drink because the ice will be broken and will retain the flavor of the previous drink. And we can't have that!

Inspired by my former home at FIFTY, **Spicy Fifty** is sweet and sour with a warm kick at the end. ❯ ❯ ❯

measurements

It is best to use a double-ended jigger when making cocktails because it helps you measure the specific amount of spirit, liqueur, or juice stated in a recipe.

Jiggers come in many sizes. Look for one whose cups measure 1 oz, 1½ oz, or 2 oz, ideally with smaller measurements marked inside one end.

The recipes in this book are given in ounces for American readers, as well as in centiliters for readers familiar with metric measurements.

The recipes use the following Imperial-to-metric equivalents:

⅓ oz = 1 cl
½ oz = 1.5 cl
⅔ oz = 2 cl

Therefore 1 oz = 3 cl, 2 oz = 6 cl, etc.

At first, it is a good idea to use the jigger to measure exact amounts so you get a good idea of what the cocktail should taste like. As your confidence grows, you might add more of this and a dash of that to change the taste to satisfy your palate.

The things to remember are
- Be consistent and retain the proportions.
- The standard volume of a cocktail is 3 oz/15 cl.
- Tall drinks such as highballs contain no more than 8 oz/24 cl.
- Medium-size cocktails are about 5 oz/15 cl.
- A spirit served on the rocks measures about 1½ oz/4.5 cl.
- Wine servings are usually 4 to 5 oz/ 12 to 15 cl.
- A glass is always filled to a level of about three-quarters, never all the way.

bar terms

Following is a list of terms that you will come across in the recipes.

APERITIF
A cocktail served before dinner to stimulate the appetite.

BLEND
To use an electric blender to make a smooth liquid from fruit, juice, coconut cream, or cream.

BRUT
Dry (when referring to Champagne).

BUILD
To pour the ingredients directly into a mixing or serving glass.

DASH
A small amount that flows when a bottle is quickly inverted once.

DIGESTIF
A cocktail served after dinner to aid digestion.

FLAME
To apply the flame of a lighter or match to a citrus twist to release the oils and lightly toast them before using the twist as a garnish.

FLOAT
To layer one spirit or liqueur over another, according to density.

FROSTED GLASS
A glass that has been chilled in the freezer.

FROSTED/CRUSTED RIM
A rim that has been salted or sugared.

MUDDLE
To crush ingredients with vigor.

NEAT
A drink served "straight," without any ice, water, or mixer.

ON THE ROCKS
A drink served on ice cubes.

PROOF
American description of alcohol content. For example, 100 proof is 50 percent alcohol by volume.

SHAKE
To use a cocktail shaker to combine all the ingredients.

SHORT DRINK
A cocktail served in an old-fashioned glass.

STIR
To mix ingredients in a mixing glass.

SPIRAL
A thin rind of orange, lemon, or lime cut horizontally around the fruit and used as a garnish.

TALL DRINK
Served in a highball with ice and measuring 8 oz/24 cl at most.

TWIST
A thin, long strip of peel twisted in the middle and dropped into the drink.

ZEST
A strip of lemon or orange peel.

TRUE
SPIRITS

base flavors for cocktails

T aking a bottle of chilled vodka from the freezer, I looked at the liquid inside the frosted bottle. The texture was viscous and the vodka was entirely colorless. How, I wondered, was I going to write about the flavor of something so innocuous? I managed to bring my vodka "flavor memory bank" to the surface and, as you will see on page 42, there was something to talk about. Of the spirits in this chapter, vodka is the one that "disappears" when mixed with other ingredients—it is intended to be all but flavorless, a chameleon, which is mostly the reason for its unassailable position as the leading spirit in the world. Brandy, Scotch, and bourbon whiskey, on the other hand, are full of flavors ranging from dark and oaky to fruity. These spirits retain their own flavor when mixed with another ingredient and come through as the underlying, lingering note. On pages 32 and 44 I elaborate on them.

The lack of a color in gin is another deception in the field of flavor. Depending on the brand, gin can dazzle the taste buds in a hundred ways. It's all in the mix of botanicals used to flavor the spirit, kept secret by the major distillers. Gin does lend its own flavor to a cocktail, hence the success of the classic gin Martini, dating back to the late nineteenth century when Jerry "The Professor" Thomas mixed his first batch. Of course, the gin they drank back then was far, far different from what is manufactured today. There is a lot more about gin on page 36.

Rums, which are made from sugarcane, have an underlying sweetness, but again, the flavors of individual rums are different, depending on the area from which they come and other factors. When you open the bottle, is the sound of a merengue or a salsa released, as well as dazzling rays of sunshine? Not quite, but some rums do cause a fun flavor sensation. On page 38 you can learn more about this primarily Caribbean and Latin American flavor.

Tequila is another fascinating spirit that's fast catching up with rum and vodka in sales. Perhaps it is the image tequila has had as the thing to drink quickly to get drunk quickly: tequila shot, lemon, and salt—lick, suck, and swallow were the actions. Tequila has grown up, as have the people who once drank those shots. More regulations governing the quality of the many tequilas that come out of Mexico have helped the flavor and its image. Buy quality tequilas and you will appreciate even more the true essence of the nation that produces them. Turn to page 40 to embrace the 100 percent agave spirit.

Sake, not a spirit but a beverage brewed from rice, is gaining affection in both cocktail and restaurant bars. The more we eat Japanese food, the more we are turning to Japanese beverages. Sake is graded according to how much the rice grains are milled before fermentation; this milling and other factors of sake-making bring a wide range of flavors to the mouth. Sake cocktails begin on page 46.

In the pages that follow, you will discover some classics and some new recipes destined to add more layers to your memory palate.

brandy

Brandy is a generic term that describes a spirit distilled from wine made from grapes or other fruits. Brandies are made all over the world from many different fruits. The most famous brandy is Cognac, from the Charente-Maritime region in France. The grapes used to make Cognac are Ugni Blanc, Folle Blanche, and Colombard. These are fermented into wine and then the wine is distilled twice and matured in oak barrels to mellow the fiery spirit and give it color. Batches of different ages and flavors are then blended to create the final product. Aromas and flavors to look for in a quality Cognac include aged Port wine, coffee, Havana cigar leaves, woody, earthy, crème brulée, licorice, honey, truffle notes, spicy, hazelnut, oak, and hints of pear.

Armagnac is a grape brandy made in Gascony, in the southwestern corner of France, from the same primary grapes used in Cognac. Distillation takes place in a type of column still, and Armagnac is distilled only once, resulting in brandy with a more rustic, fuller character and aroma than that of Cognac. Flavors to look for include dried tropical fruit, brown spices, pepper, toffee, charred nuts, raisins, smoky oak, earth, and dark caramel.

Non-grape brandies include clear eaux-de-vie such as Poire Williams (made from pears), mirabelle (made from plums), and kirsch (from cherries).

The French region of Normandy is apple country, and the cider made there can be distilled into an apple brandy known as Calvados. In the United States, apple brandy is known as applejack, while apple brandies that are similar to an eau-de-vie are made in California and Oregon. In Calvados, look for flavors of musty apples, oak, earth, and some honey, and a well-rounded finish.

| ARMAGNAC | | COGNAC | |

ARMAGNAC

Charlie's Nightcap

| 1½ oz / 4.5 cl | Armagnac |
| ½ oz / 1.5 cl | pear liqueur |

Combine the ingredients in a mixing glass with ice and stir. Strain into a brandy snifter.

D'Artagnan II

2 oz / 6 cl	Armagnac
½ oz / 1.5 cl	Grand Marnier
dash	fresh orange juice

GARNISH twist of orange

Combine the ingredients in a shaker with ice. Shake and strain into an old-fashioned glass filled with ice. Add the garnish.

COGNAC

Brandy Crusta

1½ oz / 4.5 cl	Cognac or other brandy
⅓ oz / 1 cl	orange curaçao
⅓ oz / 1 cl	maraschino liqueur
⅓ oz / 1 cl	fresh lemon juice
	superfine (caster) sugar
	wedge of lemon

GARNISH lemon spiral

Use the sugar and the wedge of lemon to crust a small goblet (see page 14). Combine the rest of the ingredients in a shaker with ice and shake. Strain into the prepared glass. Add the garnish.

Cognac Frappé

| 2 oz / 6 cl | Cognac |

Fill a brandy snifter with crushed ice and add the Cognac. Serve with a straw (optional).

The Original Sazerac

1²⁄₃ oz / 6 cl	Cognac
2 dashes	Peychaud's bitters
1 dash	Angostura bitters
1 lump	sugar
GARNISH	large lemon peel

Muddle the sugar and the bitters in the bottom of an old-fashioned glass. Add half the Cognac and two ice cubes. Stir for at least a minute, until the sugar dissolves. Add two more ice cubes and the remaining Cognac. Stir for one minute, then add two more ice cubes and stir again. Add the garnish.

Sidecar

1²⁄₃ oz / 5 cl	Cognac
³⁄₄ oz / 2.5 cl	Cointreau
½ oz / 1.5 cl	fresh lemon juice
GARNISH	maraschino cherry

Combine the ingredients in a shaker with ice and shake. Strain into a cocktail glass and add the garnish.

CALVADOS

AJ II

2 oz / 6 cl	Calvados
½ oz / 1.5 cl	fresh apple juice
dash	simple syrup (page 20)

Combine the ingredients in a shaker with ice and shake. Strain into a chilled cocktail glass.

Calvados Cocktail

2 oz / 6 cl	Calvados
½ oz / 1.5 cl	Cointreau
½ oz / 1.5 cl	orange juice

Combine the ingredients in a shaker with ice and shake. Strain into a chilled cocktail glass.

Brandy Crusta is the very first sour cocktail from 1850. ❯ ❯ ❯

gin

Gin is a spirit that is full of character. It's made with a number of botanical ingredients that stimulate and enliven the palate, keeping it fresh and clean.

The classic gin flavoring is juniper; this is used in most gins, but there are dozens of other seeds, fruits, roots, peels, and oils (the botanicals) that contribute flavor in the different styles of gin. The most common style is London Dry, which is light and aromatic—just what most people expect from gin. Recently, though, an array of exotic, international-style gins designed to lure vodka drinkers has hit the top shelf. For example, there is one triple-distilled, 94-proof, small-batch gin of impressive complexity. It is manufactured with individually distilled oils of herbs and botanicals from nine different countries, including corianders from North Africa and West Asia, almonds from Java, cassia bark from tropical Africa and from China, cubeb berries from Sri Lanka, licorice from the Mediterranean, lemon from Spain, angelica from Europe and Asia, orris from southern Europe, juniper from Italy, and grains of paradise from South Africa. Now, that's some flavor!

Also available is a handcrafted gin with only a hint of juniper, along with touches of cilantro, lemon, and orange peel. Triple-distilled for a delicate flavor, it delivers a lighter, crisper taste that gin Martini purists appreciate. Plus, there is a cucumber- and rose-petal British gin for those who like to be different.

When used in cocktails, the botanicals in gin cut through the sweetness of liqueurs and sugar. However, gin also enhances fruit flavors, in much the same way a squeeze of lemon does, without altering the flavor profile.

Gibson

2½ oz / 7.5 cl	gin
dash	dry vermouth

GARNISH white pearl onion

Pour the gin into a mixing glass filled with ice. Add the dry vermouth and stir. Strain into a chilled cocktail glass and add the garnish.

Gin Martini

2 oz / 6 cl	dry gin
½ oz / 1.5 cl	dry vermouth

GARNISH twist of lemon or an olive

Combine the ingredients in a mixing glass with ice and stir at least 15 times. Strain into a chilled cocktail glass and add the garnish.

My Martini

2½ oz / 7.5 cl	frozen gin
3 or 4 drops	dry vermouth

GARNISH lemon twist or olive

Pour the frozen gin directly into a frozen cocktail glass. Float the vermouth over the gin. If serving with a twist of lemon, rub the lemon twist around the rim of the glass, then drop it into the drink. An olive should be served on a cocktail stick.

Some say **My Martini**—so super dry, so super cool—is the best in the world! ❯ ❯ ❯

Pink Gin

2 oz / 6 cl	gin
dash	Angostura bitters
	chilled mineral water
	(optional)

Combine the gin and bitters in a mixing glass with ice and stir. Strain into an old-fashioned glass (no ice). Serve with a glass of chilled water on the side.

rum

Search through a bar's cocktail list and you'll discover an array of classic, fresh fruit-infused, or muddled cocktails made with a rum base.

Here is a nectar generally made from molasses, a sugarcane by-product. Its origins are in the Caribbean, but rum is distilled wherever sugarcane is grown. After distillation, rums are usually aged in oak casks for anywhere from a few months to thirty years or more. During the aging process, rum turns from light golden to dark brown. (Light/white rum has any color removed during the filtering process, which is just before bottling.)

There are several types of rum: light/white, golden, dark, premium aged, spiced, and overproof. To these, add the spirit cachaça, a pure sugarcane rum made only in Brazil. It is the base of the über-famous cocktail the Caipirinha.

The very dark, rich-tasting demerara rum from Guyana is made by adding spices and fruit to the mix. Rums from Haiti and Martinique are made with sugarcane juice and have a smooth finish.

Rums are a favorite of bartenders because they mix easily with tropical fruits and other flavors. However, the spirit's flavor is interesting, and you don't want to bury it by being overzealous with the other flavors. Dark or light, spiced or not, rum goes with cola, coffee, and fruits such as coconut, mango, banana, pineapple, and papaya.

Adjectives used to describe the flavor of rum are simple: sweet, caramel, vanilla, almond, floral, and banana. A lingering finish on the palate will have hints of sugarcane and oak.

The latest trend for flavored spirits has not passed rum by. Watermelon, coconut, lemon, banana, cherry, orange, and vanilla spice are just a few of the flavored rums available. Yo, ho, ho!

Black Dog

2 oz / 6 cl	light rum
dash	dry vermouth
GARNISH	black olive

Combine the ingredients in a mixing glass filled with ice and stir. Strain into a chilled cocktail glass. Add the garnish.

Rum Crusta

2 oz / 6 cl	dark rum
2 dashes	fresh lime juice
dash	Angostura bitters
	superfine (caster) sugar
	wedge of lime
GARNISH	lemon spiral

Use the sugar and the wedge of lime to crust a small wine glass (see page 14). Combine all the ingredients in a mixing glass with ice and stir. Strain into the prepared glass and add the garnish.

Rum Flame

2 oz / 6 cl	dark rum
2 or 3 dashes	orange liqueur
½ oz / 1.5 cl	overproof rum
GARNISH	orange twist

Pour the rum and the orange liqueur into a mixing glass filled with ice. Stir until cold, strain into an old-fashioned glass, and float the overproof rum on top. Flame it for a few seconds, extinguish, add ice, and stir. Garnish with a twist of orange and a cherry.

Rum in the Old Fashioned Way

2 oz / 6 cl	aged rum
dash	Angostura bitters
1	sugar cube
GARNISH	twist of lime, twist of orange

Place sugar in an old-fashioned glass and soak it with the bitters. Add enough rum to cover the cube, then crush the cube with the back of a bar spoon. Add the remaining rum and ice. Stir. Add the garnishes.

tequila

Tequila is distilled from the fermented juice of the blue agave, a succulent plant found all over Mexico, although true tequila may be produced only in designated zones. The spirit has progressed from being a basic distilled product to being a refined and sought-after connoisseur's liquor.

The character of a tequila is determined primarily by whether the spirit is 100 percent agave, whether it is aged, and for how long it is aged. This spirit gains color, aroma, and flavor from the barrels used for aging. The flavor differs, depending on how long the tequila has been aged: blanco/silver (essentially unaged), gold (a blanco with caramel added for color and flavor), reposado ("rested" for two to twelve months), or añejo ("aged" for one to three years). Whichever type you drink, it will seduce you with its subtle fragrances and traditional dusky aromas.

In a blanco/silver style, you might find lime, citrus, pear with an herbal note, and spiciness balanced with an earthy tone. Sometimes you'll get a hint of vanilla. Añejo tequilas, made from 100 percent blue agave, should be smooth, dark, and rich, bourbon-like in color and flavor.

Some artisanal tequilas have delicate, floral flavors such as a hint of eucalyptus and peppermint in a blanco, or fruitiness and tobacco in an añejo. Triple-distilled tequilas are intense with agave flavor.

Classic Tequila Shot

1 oz / 3 cl	gold tequila
pinch	salt
	wedge of lime

Pour the tequila into a shot glass. Hold the wedge of lime between your index finger and thumb. Place the salt at the base of the thumb on the same hand. Quickly, lick the salt, down the tequila, and bite the lime.

Tequila Slammer

| 1²⁄₃ oz / 5 cl | añejo (aged) tequila |
| 1²⁄₃ oz / 5 cl | Champagne |

Combine the tequila and Champagne in an old-fashioned glass with a heavy base. Hold a napkin on top of the glass and slam the glass down on a table or countertop. Drink the cocktail as it fizzes. (Do this carefully, please, so you do not break the glass.)

Estilo Viejo

1¾ oz / 5 cl	añejo (aged) tequila
1 tsp	simple syrup (page 20)
6 drops	Angostura bitters
GARNISH	orange zest

Combine the simple syrup and the bitters in an old-fashioned glass. Add 1 ice cube and stir. Add half of the tequila and 2 more ice cubes. Stir for about 30 seconds. Add the rest of the tequila and 2 more ice cubes and stir well for another 30 seconds. Add more ice to fill to the rim. Rub the orange zest around the rim of the glass, squeeze it over the top of the drink to release the oils, then drop it in.

Tequila-ini

2 oz / 6 cl	añejo (aged) tequila
½ oz / 1.5 cl	dry vermouth
GARNISH	twist of lime

Combine the ingredients in a mixing glass filled with ice. Stir until cold and frosty. Strain into a chilled cocktail glass. Add the garnish.

vodka

Vodka is often thought of as flavorless, but in fact, vodkas made outside the United States often retain hints of flavor from the grain, potatoes, beets, or grapes used to distill them, as well as the water used to dilute them after distillation. The number of distillations and permitted textural ingredients create variations in mouthfeel.

The Finnish like to produce what they refer to as naked vodka, with the purity of the glacial spring water being the key to its flavor. Russian and Eastern European vodka producers contribute a variety of products whose flavors and textures result from triple distillation and then triple filtering. Vodkas flavored with fruit, vegetables, spices, and other ingredients are incredibly popular. Raspberry, black currant, orange, pomegranate, lemon, and strawberry are just a few of the fruit flavors available. Others include buffalo grass, black or chile pepper, horseradish, basil, rose, and vanilla. These are all best served simply, on the rocks or chilled straight up.

Level Martini

2 oz / 6 cl	frozen vodka
½ oz / 1.5 cl	dry sherry
1 tsp	caper juice
GARNISH	caper berry

Combine the ingredients in a mixing glass filled with ice and stir. Strain into a chilled cocktail glass. Add the garnish.

Vodka Martini

2½ oz / 7.5 cl	frozen vodka
2 dashes	extra dry vermouth
GARNISH	twist of lemon or green olive

Pour the vodka into a chilled cocktail glass. Float the vermouth over the top. Add the twist of lemon or drop an olive in the glass.

A **Level Martini** has an interesting, slightly salty taste from the caper juice. ❯ ❯ ❯

whiskey

A merican whiskey and Scotch offer complex flavors that ignite staunch loyalties among those who prefer one or another flavor profile.

A number of styles of whiskey are made in the United States, but bourbon is the best-known. Bourbon must be distilled from fermented grain mash comprised of at least 51 percent corn. The whiskey is then aged in charred new oak barrels. Some say that the color, caramel, smoke, and vanilla flavors plus the tannic nip in bourbons are there because of the charring inside the barrels. Other flavors include spice, floral accents, light to medium honey, apricots, cloves, charcoal, citrus, hazelnut, malt, nutmeg, oak, pepper, and maple syrup. Types of bourbon include blended, single barrel, small batch, and special aged.

There are five categories of Scotch whisky: single malt, single grain, blended malt, blended Scotch, and blended-grain Scotch. Blended Scotch may contain up to 40 or 50 different Scotch whiskies selected for their character, flavor, and bouquet. In general terms, Scotch whisky can present soft and malty flavors, zesty-oak and warm peat-smoke notes, fresh nutmeg and toasted almonds; it can also be faintly salty and intensely peaty. Claret, dark chocolate, licorice, peach, brown sugar, and tangerine flavors are also found in Scotch.

Excellent blended whiskies are also produced in Canada, and both blended and single-malt whiskies are made in Ireland and Japan—all with their devoted following.

In cocktails, dark spirits hold their own when other flavors are added. For instance, in a Rusty Nail the earthy flavor of the Scotch is not overcome by the Drambuie liqueur. The Scotch holds its own as a good Scotch should. Blended bourbon and Scotch, rather than single barrel or single malt, are most commonly used in cocktails.

Manhattan

1⅔ oz / 5 cl	rye or Canadian Club whisky
⅔ oz / 2 cl	sweet vermouth
2 dashes	Angostura bitters
GARNISH	maraschino cherry

Combine the ingredients in a mixing glass with ice and stir. Strain into a chilled cocktail glass. Add the garnish.

New Orleans

2 oz / 6 cl	bourbon
2 dashes	orange curaçao
3 dashes	Peychaud's bitters
GARNISH	orange peel

Combine the ingredients in a mixing glass with ice and stir. Strain into a chilled cocktail glass. Add the garnish.

Old Fashioned

2 oz / 6 cl	bourbon
dash	Angostura bitters
1	sugar cube
	club soda
GARNISH	half-slice of orange, maraschino cherry

Place the sugar cube in the base of an old-fashioned glass. Soak with bitters and a dash of club soda. Crush the sugar with the back of a bar spoon. Add half the bourbon and two ice cubes and stir until the sugar is dissolved. Add more ice and the remaining bourbon and stir. Add the garnish. Serve with a stirrer.

Rusty Nail

2 oz / 6 cl	Scotch
1 oz / 3 cl	Drambuie
GARNISH	twist of lemon

Combine the ingredients in an old-fashioned glass filled with ice and stir. Add the garnish.

The king of old whisky cocktails is, without a doubt, the **Old Fashioned**. ❯ ❯ ❯

sake

S ake is fermented from rice, and although it is often called "rice wine," it is
more like a beer in terms of the process used to make it. Sake is not
carbonated, however, and more resembles wine in flavor. It is not a distilled
beverage and is not related to gin, vodka, or light rum in any way, yet it can,
and does, replace these clear spirits in some adventurous cocktail recipes.

This exotic liquor can be sipped warm or room temperature or taken chilled.
Most people know its warmth, but in a cocktail with other ingredients, it takes on a
different life.

The fermented rice ingredient is very important to sake's flavor. It can provide
a hint of pineapple, coconut, or tropical fruit in general. Filtered dry sakes are used to
make stiffer drinks.

If you get the opportunity to taste a sake before you buy, look for balance in the
flavors. Nothing should be cloying or pushy in the flavor. A sake can be quite dry and
even acidic, or quite sweet, and still be in harmony. If it is dull and sickly-sweet or harsh,
try another brand. A gentle hint of fruit and a balanced sweetness are good.

Blue Rain

1²⁄₃ oz / 5 cl	sake
²⁄₃ oz / 2 cl	pear liqueur
¹⁄₃ oz / 1 cl	blue curaçao
¹⁄₃ oz / 1 cl	fresh lemon juice
GARNISH	wedge of pear

Combine the ingredients in a shaker with ice and shake. Strain into a chilled cocktail glass. Slit the pear wedge and place it on the rim of the glass.

Hong Kong

2 oz / 6 cl	sake
²⁄₃ oz / 2 cl	red vermouth
dash	Campari
2 dashes	Angostura bitters
GARNISH	twist of lemon

Combine the ingredients in a shaker with ice and shake. Strain into a chilled cocktail glass. Add the garnish.

Pink Bamboo

1½ oz / 4.5 cl	aged sake
1½ oz / 4.5 cl	rosé vermouth
¹⁄₃ oz / 1 cl	maraschino liqueur
dash	mandarin bitters
GARNISH	pink rose petal

Combine the ingredients in a mixing glass with ice and stir. Strain into a chilled cocktail glass. Add the garnish.

Sparkling Sakepom

1½ oz / 4.5 cl	sake
1 oz / 3 cl	pomegranate juice
dash	grenadine
	Champagne
1 tsp	cayenne
1 tsp	superfine (caster) sugar
	wedge of lemon

Combine the cayenne and sugar on a plate and use the mixture, with the wedge of lemon, to crust a chilled cocktail glass (see page 14). Combine the sake, pomegranate juice, and grenadine in a shaker with ice and shake. Strain into the cocktail glass. Top up with Champagne. Stir.

A TO Z OF
FLAVORS

bitters

itters fall into two basic categories: cocktail bitters and digestive bitters. Cocktail bitters are generally unsweetened and are used a dash or two at a time in cocktail mixology. Angostura and Peychaud's (an orange-flavored bitters produced in New Orleans) are the brands used in this book. Digestive bitters are usually sweetened and are consumed after dinner to aid the digestion. They are also becoming more and more common as cocktail ingredients.

In the classic cocktail sense, the word *bitters* is associated with bitter flavors created by combining herbs, roots, and other botanicals. Bitters date back to pre-Medieval times, when herbalists mixed up medications from these ingredients. Eventually, the bitterness was disguised by the addition of sugar. Smelling some of these mixtures in the bottle might make you wrinkle your nose at the unfamiliar, earthy aromas. However, once you have braved a sip, you might surprise yourself and develop a taste for them.

The body needs bitter foods to stimulate various metabolic processes associated with cleansing the liver and the digestive system. This in turn helps the body better assimilate vitamins and minerals. Hangover cures use bitters, and when your stomach isn't in the best condition, bitters such as Fernet Branca, Underberg, or Jägermeister are useful drinks. Often these family-originated herbal recipes are kept secret. For instance, Jägermeister is made from a mixture of fifty-six roots, barks, blossoms, and herbs that are macerated, blended, stored in wooden vats, and filtered before bottling.

Bitter flavors also stimulate the appetite, a reason bitters are popular in pre-dinner cocktails. Some bitter flavors can be a shock to the palate, but the upside is that bitters tend to contain less sugar than other spirits or liqueurs. Bitter cocktail ingredients include almond liqueur, tonic water, Campari, Punt e Mes, Aperol, Cynar, anis, and Pernod, as well as the previously mentioned cocktail bitters and digestives. Traditionally used in many of the early classic cocktail recipes, some older brands are undergoing a modern makeover as their owners attempt to capture the palates of the youth market, people who have grown up on sweet colas. This is a challenge but surely a worthwhile one.

In the recipes that follow, you will discover some classics and some newer combinations designed to improve your digestion and educate your palate.

APEROL

Bella Taormina

1 oz / 3 cl	gin
⅔ oz / 2 cl	Aperol
½ oz / 1.5 cl	limoncello
½ oz / 1.5 cl	Mandarine Napoleon liqueur
⅔ oz / 2 cl	fresh orange juice
GARNISH	lime spiral

Combine the ingredients in a shaker with ice and shake. Strain into a chilled cocktail glass. Add the garnish.

Friends

1 oz / 3 cl	Aperol
1 oz / 3 cl	gin
1 oz / 3 cl	dry vermouth
GARNISH	twist of lemon

Combine the ingredients in a mixing glass filled with ice and stir. Strain into a chilled cocktail glass. Twist the lemon peel over the drink, then drop it in.

Gillia

2 oz / 6 cl	Aperol
1 oz / 3 cl	Scotch whisky
GARNISH	twist of orange

Combine the ingredients in a mixing glass with ice and stir. Strain into a chilled cocktail glass. Add the garnish.

CAMPARI

Amico

1⅓ oz / 4 cl	tequila
1 oz / 3 cl	Campari
1 oz / 3 cl	pink grapefruit juice
½ oz / 1.5 cl	fresh lime juice
½ oz / 1.5 cl	agave syrup
GARNISH	wedge of grapefruit

Combine the ingredients in a shaker with ice and shake. Strain into an old-fashioned glass filled with ice. Add the garnish.

Bloodhound

2 oz / 6 cl	Campari
1 oz / 3 cl	vodka
	fresh grapefruit juice
GARNISH	half a slice of grapefruit

Pour the Campari and vodka into a highball filled with ice. Top with grapefruit juice and stir. Garnish with half a grapefruit slice dropped in the drink.

Blushing Fran

1⅓ oz / 4 cl	vodka
½ oz / 1.5 cl	Campari
½ oz / 1.5 cl	Framboise liqueur
½ oz / 1.5 cl	elderflower cordial
⅓ oz / 1 cl	fresh lemon juice
½ slice	fresh pineapple, cut into chunks
2	thin slices red chile pepper
	superfine (caster) sugar
	wedge of lemon
GARNISH	small red-eye chile

Use the sugar and the wedge of lemon to crust a chilled cocktail glass (see page 14). Muddle the pineapple in the bottom of the shaker. Add ice and the remaining ingredients and shake hard to bruise the chile. Double-strain into the prepared glass. Slit the red-eye chile and place it on the rim of the glass.

Brother

1⅓ oz / 4 cl	tequila
1 oz / 3 cl	Campari
1 oz / 3 cl	pink grapefruit juice
½ oz / 1.5 cl	fresh lime juice
½ oz / 1.5 cl	agave syrup
GARNISH	wedge of grapefruit

Combine the ingredients in a shaker with ice and shake. Strain into an old-fashioned glass filled with ice. Add the garnish.

Campari Nobile

1 oz / 3 cl	vodka
⅔ oz / 2 cl	Campari
1 oz / 3 cl	limoncello
2⅓ oz / 7 cl	orange juice
1 oz / 3 cl	raspberry puree
	bitter lemon
GARNISH	2 raspberries, mint leaf, slice of orange

Combine all the ingredients except the bitter lemon in a shaker with ice and shake. Strain into a highball filled with ice. Top up with bitter lemon and stir. Slit the orange and place it on the rim of the glass. Place the berries and mint in the drink. Serve with a straw and a stirrer.

Diamond Dog

1 oz / 3 cl	Campari
1 oz / 3 cl	dry vermouth
1 oz / 3 cl	Rose's lime juice
1 oz / 3 cl	fresh orange juice
GARNISH	slice of orange

Combine the ingredients in a shaker with ice and shake. Strain into an old-fashioned glass filled with ice. Add the garnish.

Diana's Bitter

1⅓ oz / 4 cl	Plymouth gin
⅔ oz / 2 cl	Campari
⅔ oz / 2 cl	fresh lime juice
½ oz / 1.5 cl	simple syrup (page 20)
GARNISH	wedge of lime

Combine the ingredients in a shaker with ice and shake. Strain into a chilled cocktail glass. Add the garnish.

Garibaldi

1⅔ oz / 5 cl	Campari
3⅓ oz / 10 cl	fresh orange juice
GARNISH	half slice of orange

Pour the Campari into an old-fashioned glass filled with ice. Add the orange juice and stir. Add the garnish.

Maiori Magic

1⅓ oz / 4 cl	Campari
⅔ oz / 2 cl	limoncello
⅔ oz / 2 cl	fresh lemon juice
	tonic water
GARNISH	wedge of lemon

Pour the Campari, limoncello, and lemon juice into a highball filled with ice. Top up with tonic water and stir. Squeeze a wedge of lemon over the drink, then drop it in.

Marked Man

1½ oz / 4.5 cl	Maker's Mark bourbon
½ oz / 1.5 cl	Campari
½ oz / 1.5 cl	limoncello
½ oz / 1.5 cl	orange juice
3	fresh mint leaves
1	slice ginger
GARNISH	few sticks of ginger

Muddle the mint and slice of ginger in the bottom of a shaker. Add ice and remaining ingredients and shake well. Strain into a chilled cocktail glass. Balance the garnish on the rim of the glass.

Monza

1 oz / 3 cl	vodka
1 oz / 3 cl	Campari
3 oz / 9 cl	apple juice
dash	simple syrup (page 20)
1	passion fruit
GARNISH	apple fan (page 15) and mint tip

Scoop the flesh of the passion fruit into a shaker. Add remaining ingredients and ice and shake. Strain into highball filled with ice, allowing some of the fruit to filter through for texture. Add the garnish.

Negroni

1 oz / 3 cl	Campari
1 oz / 3 cl	gin
1 oz / 3 cl	sweet vermouth
GARNISH	quarter slice of orange

Pour the Campari, gin, and vermouth into an old-fashioned glass filled with ice and stir. Add the garnish in the drink.

Spirit Lifter

1 oz / 3 cl	Cointreau
1 oz / 3 cl	Campari
1 oz / 3 cl	fresh orange juice

Combine the ingredients in a shaker with ice and shake. Strain into a chilled cocktail glass.

FERNET BRANCA

Apothecary Cocktail

1 oz / 3 cl	Fernet Branca
1 oz / 3 cl	white crème de menthe
1 oz / 3 cl	Punt e Mes

Combine the ingredients in a mixing glass with ice and stir. Strain into a chilled cocktail glass.

Body & Soul Reviver

1 oz / 3 cl	Branca Menthe
1 oz / 3 cl	Cognac
dash	orange bitters

Combine the ingredients in a shaker with ice and shake. Strain into a shot glass.

Corpse Reviver 3

1 oz / 3 cl	brandy
1 oz / 3 cl	white crème de menthe
1 oz / 3 cl	Fernet Branca

Combine the ingredients in a mixing glass with ice and stir. Strain into a chilled cocktail glass.

Fernet Cocktail

1 oz / 3 cl	brandy
1 oz / 3 cl	Fernet Branca
1 dash	Angostura bitters
2 dashes	simple syrup (page 20)
GARNISH	twist of lemon

Combine the ingredients in a mixing glass with ice and stir. Strain into a chilled cocktail glass. Add the garnish.

‹ ‹ ‹ A **Marked Man** has sticks of ginger as a garnish, giving a hint of spice on the nose.

fruits

This section is a celebration of fresh, seasonal, handpicked fruit that can be used to make a cocktail. Fruit has many tastes and intensities, ranging from sweet to sharp to delicate or slightly bitter. From the humble green apple and citrus fruits to summer stone fruits such as apricots and deep red cherries, the selection of fruits in these recipes is deliciously tempting.

Seasonal delights abound in nature's food year, so always look for the freshest fruits at your local farmer's market or quality supermarket. In cocktails, freshness means the finest flavor. If the fruit is in a basket or covered in plastic, look through the container as best you can to ensure that no moldy pieces of fruit are hidden away on the bottom. Wash fruit such as strawberries, blueberries, blackberries, apples, and pears, and pat dry before using them in cocktails. Raspberries don't respond well to being washed, so try to find fresh berries that have not been sprayed.

When fruit is to be used in a cocktail, the recipe will require you either to muddle the fruit in the bottom of a shaker or a heavy-bottomed glass (see page 11), or to blend the ingredients until smooth. After blending fruit, you may wish to place it in a muslin cloth to strain out any unwanted fiber or seeds. In a few cases, fresh fruit is shaken vigorously in a cocktail shaker, so the ice bruises the fruit and releases its juices.

When fresh fruit is not in season, canned fruit or juice may be used to replace the real thing, but these ingredients will result in a cocktail with a different flavor. If possible, use frozen fruit puree.

Before you order a drink, consider whether the fruit in the cocktail recipe is in season. If it's not, try a flavor that is—you might discover something new.

In the pages that follow, you will find some superb fruit-flavored cocktails that offer more than a little pleasure for the palate.

açaí berry

The Amazon's açaí is the newest berry to hit the market and is packed with much more antioxidant power than red grapes. The flavor is hard to pinpoint. The flavor of some brands of juice has been compared to bitter raspberry with a hint of cocoa bean.

Açaí Martini

1²/₃ oz / 5 cl	vodka
²/₃ oz / 2 cl	triple sec
1 oz / 3 cl	açaí berry juice

Combine the ingredients in a shaker with ice and shake. Strain into a chilled cocktail glass.

Açaí Punch *serves 4*

8 oz / 24 cl	red wine
2 pts / 75 cl	açaí berry juice
3 oz / 9 cl	orange juice
1 each	lime, lemon, orange, sliced
6	fresh mint sprigs
	soda water
GARNISH	sprig of mint

Combine the wine, açaí juice, and citrus slices in a large pitcher with 2 sprigs of mint and stir. Refrigerate for an hour. Just before you are ready to serve, add the orange juice and a large scoop of crushed ice. Stir. Serve in a highball. Top up with a little soda water and add a sprig of mint to each glass.

Zenith

1 oz / 3 cl	lemon vodka
½ oz / 1.5 cl	green tea liqueur
⅓ oz / 1 cl	fresh lemon juice
1 oz / 3 cl	açaí berry juice
GARNISH	lemongrass stick, twist of lemon

Combine the ingredients in a shaker with ice and shake. Strain into a chilled cocktail glass. Add the garnish.

apple

Granny Smith, Golden Delicious, and Braeburn varieties are good to use in cocktails because of their balance of sweet and sour flavors. Look for firm, juicy flesh and crispness. Apples go well with brandy, Calvados, cinnamon, blackberries, and vanilla.

Apple Crumble

1¾ oz / 5 cl	reposado tequila
¾ oz / 2.5 cl	heavy (double) cream
1¾ oz / 5 cl	fresh apple cider
dash	fresh lime juice
1¾ oz / 5 cl	apple puree
½ oz / 1.5 cl	cinnamon syrup (page 20)
GARNISH	oatmeal cookie crumbs

Combine all the ingredients except the cream in a shaker with ice and shake. Strain into an old-fashioned glass filled with ice. Rest the wrong end of a bar spoon on the surface of the drink and slowly pour the cream down the twisted handle so it forms a thin layer on top of the drink. Garnish with a sprinkle of cookie crumbs.

Apple Daiquiri

1½ oz / 4.5 cl	light rum
1 oz / 3 cl	fresh apple juice
½ oz / 1.5 cl	fresh lime juice
⅓ oz / 1 cl	simple syrup (page 20)
GARNISH	wedge of lime

Combine the ingredients in a shaker with ice and shake. Strain into a chilled cocktail glass. Slit the lime and place it on the rim of the glass.

Apple Pie Martini

1½ oz / 4.5 cl	Zubrowka bison grass vodka
½ oz / 1.5 cl	Goldschläger cinnamon schnapps
1½ oz / 4.5 cl	fresh apple juice
½ oz / 1.5 cl	cranberry juice
GARNISH	apple fan (page 15)

Combine the ingredients in a shaker with ice and shake. Strain into a chilled cocktail glass and add the garnish.

Applik Delight, with a velvety texture and fresh apple aroma, gets a gentle kick from ginger marmalade. ❱ ❱ ❱

Apple-tini

2 oz / 6 cl	vodka
⅔ oz / 2 cl	sour apple liqueur
1/3 oz / 1 cl	Cointreau
GARNISH	apple fan (page 15)

Combine the ingredients in a shaker with ice and shake. Strain into a chilled cocktail glass. Add the garnish on the rim.

Appleton Garden

2 oz / 6 cl	rum
1 oz / 3 cl	sweet vermouth
1 oz / 3 cl	fresh lime juice
4 oz / 12 cl	apple juice
GARNISH	ground cinnamon

Combine the ingredients in a shaker with ice and shake. Strain into a highball filled with ice. Sprinkle freshly ground cinnamon on top of the drink.

Applik Delight

1⅔ oz / 5 cl	Stoli Gala Applik
1 tsp	Edmond Briottet Liqueur au Coquelicot de Nemours (poppy liqueur) or Framboise
1 oz / 3 cl	fresh Gala apple juice
½ oz / 1.5 cl	fresh lemon juice
1½ tsps	ginger marmalade
GARNISH	red apple fan (page 15)

Combine the ingredients in a shaker and stir well to dissolve the marmalade. Add ice and shake. Double-strain into a chilled cocktail glass and add the garnish.

Va-Va-Voom

1⅔ oz / 5 oz	vodka
½ oz / 1.5 cl	passion fruit syrup (page 22)
3 oz / 9 cl	apple juice
½ oz / 1.5 cl	lime juice
4	fresh mint leaves
GARNISH	apple fan (page 15), sprig of mint

Combine the ingredients in a shaker with ice and shake hard to bruise the mint. Strain into a highball filled with crushed ice. Add the garnish.

apricot

The flavor of this small and perfectly formed fruit is sweet and honeyed, with lush flesh designed to melt in the mouth. The fragrance is elegant. Use apricot liqueur or juice with saffron, vanilla, hazelnut liqueur, and chocolate.

Apricot Cosmo

1⅔ oz / 5 cl	vodka
½ oz / 1.5 cl	apricot brandy
½ oz / 1.5 cl	cranberry juice
½ oz / 1.5 cl	fresh lime juice
1 tsp	apricot jam

GARNISH   twist of orange

Combine the ingredients in a shaker with ice and shake. Strain into a chilled cocktail glass. Add the garnish.

Apricot Sour

1 oz / 3 cl	vodka
1 oz / 3 cl	apricot brandy
1 oz / 3 cl	fresh lemon juice
2 tsps	apricot jam
dash	egg white

GARNISH   slivers of dried apricot

Combine the ingredients in a shaker with ice and shake. Strain into a chilled cocktail glass. Drop the slivers of dried apricot on top of the drink.

Lady Apricot

1 oz / 3 cl	gin
1 oz / 3 cl	apricot brandy
1 oz / 3 cl	fresh lime juice
½ oz / 1.5 cl	simple syrup (page 20)
1	egg white

GARNISH   wedge of apricot, sprig of mint

Combine the ingredients in a shaker with ice and shake. Strain into an old-fashioned glass filled with ice. Add the garnish.

‹ ‹ ‹ **Va-Va-Voom** shows off an apple fan.

Madagascar Sour

2 oz / 6 cl	light rum
1 oz / 3 cl	fresh lemon juice
dash	peach bitters
1 tsp	apricot preserves
1	egg white
1 tsp	superfine (caster) sugar
½	vanilla bean

GARNISH   apricot half

Muddle the vanilla bean in the bottom of a shaker. Add ice and the remaining ingredients and shake. Double-strain into an old-fashioned glass filled with ice. Slit the apricot and place it on the rim of the glass.

Naked Lady

1 oz / 3 cl	light rum
1 oz / 3 cl	apricot brandy
½ oz / 1.5 cl	fresh lemon juice
dash	grenadine

GARNISH   maraschino cherry

Combine the ingredients in a shaker with ice and shake. Strain into a chilled cocktail glass. Add the garnish.

Southern Sea Breeze

1½ oz / 4.5 cl	bourbon
⅔ oz / 2 cl	apricot brandy
½ oz / 1.5 cl	fresh lemon juice
2	dried apricots
1	dried fig
dash	simple syrup (page 20)

GARNISH   dried apricot, fig

Muddle the apricots, fig, and simple syrup in the bottom of a shaker. Add the remaining ingredients and ice and shake well. Double-strain into an old-fashioned glass filled with ice. Garnish with small pieces of dried apricot and fig skewered on a toothpick and placed across the top of the glass.

‹ ‹ ‹ **Apricot Sour** combines sweet and sour flavors with a smooth finish from the apricot.

banana

The flavor of this small and perfectly formed fruit is sweet
and honeyed, with lush flesh designed to melt in the mouth.
The fragrance is elegant. Use apricot liqueur or juice
with saffron, vanilla, hazelnut liqueur, and chocolate.

Banana Batida

2 oz / 6 cl	cachaça
1 oz / 3 cl	crème de banane
½ oz / 1.5 cl	fresh lime juice
1	banana, peeled
GARNISH	slice of banana, maraschino cherry

Combine the ingredients in a blender and
blend until smooth. Add a scoop of crushed
ice. Blend for 10 seconds more. Pour into a
highball and add the garnish. Serve with
a straw.

Banana Blaze

1⅔ oz / 5 cl	Cognac
1 oz / 3 cl	crème de banane
dash	orange bitters
few	cloves
few	star anise
GARNISH	twist of orange

Place the spices in a small muslin bag and tie
securely. Combine the other ingredients in a
small saucepan and add the spices. Heat over
low heat just until hot. Remove the spices

from the pan. Pour the drink into a heatproof
glass and use a lighter to ignite the top of
the drink. Let it blaze for a few seconds, then
snuff it out. Add the garnish.

Banana Daiquiri

1⅓ oz / 4 cl	light rum
⅔ oz / 2 cl	banana liqueur
⅓ oz / 1 cl	fresh lime juice
1	banana, peeled and diced
GARNISH	small slice of banana

Combine the ingredients in a blender and
blend for 10 seconds. Add a small scoop of
crushed ice and blend again. Pour into a
chilled large cocktail glass or wine glass.
Slit the banana slice and place it on the rim
of the glass.

Banana Delight

1 oz / 3 cl	vodka
1 oz / 3 cl	crème de banane
½ oz / 1.5 cl	white crème de cacao
1 tsp	clear honey
1 oz / 3 cl	heavy (double) cream
GARNISH	single honeysuckle blossom

Combine the ingredients in a shaker with ice and shake. Strain into a chilled cocktail glass. Add the garnish.

Beach Babe

1⅔ oz / 5 cl	golden rum
½ oz / 1.5 cl	banana liqueur
2 oz / 6 cl	fresh orange juice
2 dashes	orange bitters
1	banana, peeled and diced
GARNISH	cape gooseberry

Combine the ingredients in a blender and blend until smooth. Add a scoop of crushed ice. Blend again for 10 seconds. Pour into a highball. Top up with crushed ice and stir. Add the garnish.

Slipslider

1 oz / 3 cl	crème de banane
½ oz / 1.5 cl	Frangelico
½ oz / 1.5 cl	Irish cream liqueur

Gently pour each ingredient in the order listed into a shot glass, to create a layered effect (see page 13).

White Sandy Beach (nonalcoholic)

3 oz / 9 cl	pineapple juice
1⅔ oz / 5 cl	coconut cream
½ oz / 1.5 cl	heavy (double) cream
1	small ripe banana
GARNISH	3 pieces of peeled banana, ground nutmeg

Combine the ingredients in a blender with a scoop of crushed ice and blend until smooth. Pour into a chilled tumbler. Put banana pieces on a cocktail stick, place the stick across the top of the glass, and grate a fine sprinkle of nutmeg over the drink.

blackberry

Best picked when they are plump and soft, blackberries
are delicious fresh. Blackberry liqueur (crème de mûre) is also
a desirable ingredient in a cocktail—try the Kir (page 189).

Blackberry Scramble

1¾ oz / 5 cl	silver tequila
1 oz / 3 cl	fresh lemon juice
½ oz / 1.5 cl	simple syrup (page 20)
dash	crème de mûre
GARNISH	blackberry, slice of lemon

Half-fill an old-fashioned glass with crushed
ice and pour the tequila, lemon juice, and
simple syrup over the ice. Stir. Fill to the rim
with more crushed ice. Gently pour in the
crème de mûre, creating a bleeding effect
through the drink. Slit the lemon slice and
place it on the rim of the glass. Add the
blackberry to the drink.

Black Bison

1½ oz / 4.5 cl	Zubrowka bison grass vodka
½ oz / 1.5 cl	Chambord liqueur
2 oz / 6 cl	fresh apple juice
½ oz / 1.5 cl	fresh lemon juice
5	blackberries
1 tsp	superfine (caster) sugar
GARNISH	a few blackberries, apple fan (page 15)

Muddle the blackberries and sugar in the
bottom of a shaker. Add the remaining
ingredients and ice. Shake. Double-strain
into a highball filled with crushed ice. Add
the garnish.

Blimey

1½ oz / 4.5 cl	vodka
½ oz / 1.5 cl	crème de cassis
1 oz / 3 cl	lemon juice
½ oz / 1.5 cl	simple syrup (page 20)
5	blackberries
GARNISH	blackberry

Muddle the blackberries in the bottom of a
shaker. Add ice and the remaining ingredients
and shake. Strain into an old-fashioned glass
filled with crushed ice. Add the garnish.

Bramble

1²⁄₃ oz / 5 cl	gin
¾ oz / 2.5 cl	crème de mûre
¾ oz / 2.5 cl	fresh lemon juice
½ oz / 1.5 cl	simple syrup (page 20)
GARNISH	a few blackberries

Half-fill a highball with crushed ice. Add the gin, lemon juice and simple syrup and stir. Add more crushed ice and float the crème de mûre on top by gently pouring it over the back of a bar spoon. Add the garnish.

Godfrey

1½ oz / 4.5 cl	Cognac
½ oz / 1.5 cl	Grand Marnier
½ oz / 1.5 cl	crème de mûre
⅓ oz / 1 cl	fresh lemon juice
4	blackberries
GARNISH	2 blackberries, mint leaf

Combine the ingredients in a shaker with ice and shake sharply to break down the fruit. Strain into an old-fashioned glass filled with ice, allowing some of the fruit to pass through. Add the garnish to a cocktail stick and place it on top of the drink.

Inspired by a Cognac lover, **Godfrey** offers fresh flavors with a warm finish. ❯ ❯ ❯

Sexy Spring Punch

1½ oz / 4.5 cl	vodka
½ oz / 1.5 cl	crème de mûre
½ oz / 1.5 cl	fresh lemon juice
4	blackberries
	Champagne
GARNISH	slice of lemon, blackberry

Muddle the berries in the bottom of a shaker. Add ice and the remaining ingredients except Champagne. Shake. Strain into a highball filled with ice. Top up with Champagne and stir. Add the garnish.

black currant

With a shiny purple-black skin, fresh black currants are sour and require sugar to temper their taste. However, crème de cassis, the black currant liqueur, is just sweet enough.

Back in Black

2 oz / 6 cl	black currant–infused aged rum*
⅓ oz / 1 cl	tawny Port
⅓ oz / 1 cl	crème de cassis
3 oz / 9 cl	black currant tea
	club soda

GARNISH   black currants

Make tea and let cool for 10 minutes. Combine the ingredients except the club soda in a shaker with ice and shake. Strain into a highball filled with ice. Top up with club soda. Add the garnish.

*To infuse the rum: Add 50 black currants to 325 ml (half a bottle) of aged rum. Set aside for a few days for the flavors to combine.

Black Door

1⅔ oz / 5 cl	black currant vodka
½ oz / 1.5 cl	crème de cassis
⅔ oz / 2 cl	fresh lime juice
3	black currants

GARNISH   sprig of black currants

Muddle the black currants in the bottom of a shaker. Add ice and the remaining ingredients and shake well. Strain into a chilled cocktail glass. Add the garnish on the side of the glass.

High Heel

1½ oz / 4.5 cl	vodka
½ oz / 1.5 cl	crème de cassis
dash	fresh lemon juice
6	black currants
3	raspberries

GARNISH   3 black currants

Combine the ingredients in a shaker with ice and shake hard to break down the fruit. Strain into an old-fashioned glass filled with crushed ice. Add the garnish.

Russian Spring Punch

1½ oz / 4.5 cl	vodka
⅔ oz / 2 cl	crème de cassis
½ oz / 1.5 cl	fresh lemon juice
2 dashes	simple syrup (page 20)
	Champagne

GARNISH   3 black currants

Combine the ingredients except the Champagne in a highball filled with crushed ice. Top up with Champagne and stir. Add the garnish. Serve with a straw.

blueberry

A native North American berry, the blueberry has a
plump, sweet flesh and gives great juice when muddled.
Full of antioxidants and vitamin C, the blueberry
is also thought to have anti-aging effects.

Blueberry Caipirinha

2 oz / 6 cl	cachaça
half	lime, diced
15	blueberries
1½ tsps	superfine (caster) sugar

Muddle the lime in the bottom of an old-
fashioned glass to extract the juice. Add the
blueberries and gently muddle. Add the sugar
and the cachaça. Add crushed ice and stir.
Serve with a straw.

Blueberry Muffin Martini

1 oz / 3 cl	vodka
½ oz / 1.5 cl	vanilla vodka
½ oz / 1.5 cl	blueberry liqueur
½ oz / 1.5 cl	white crème de cacao
3	fresh blueberries
GARNISH	4 blueberries, vanilla bean

Combine the ingredients in a shaker with
ice and shake hard to break down the fruit.
Double-strain into a cocktail glass. Thread the
blueberries onto the vanilla bean and place it
on the edge of the glass.

Blueberry Rocket

1½ oz / 4.5 cl	light rum
½ oz / 1.5 cl	blueberry liqueur
1 oz / 3 cl	fresh lime juice
dash	vanilla syrup (page 24)
10	blueberries
GARNISH	3 blueberries

Muddle the blueberries in the bottom of a
shaker. Add the remaining ingredients and ice
and shake sharply. Double-strain into a chilled
cocktail glass. Add the garnish.

cherry

Both sweet and sour varieties are rich in antioxidants. Maraschino and Morello sour cherries are used to make kirsch liqueur, and the maraschino is familiar as the red cocktail cherry.

Blood & Sand

1 oz / 3 cl	Scotch whisky
2/3 oz / 2 cl	cherry brandy
2/3 oz / 2 cl	sweet vermouth
2/3 oz / 2 cl	fresh blood-orange juice
GARNISH	twist of orange

Combine the ingredients in a shaker with ice and shake. Strain into a chilled cocktail glass. Twist the orange peel over the drink, then drop it in.

Cherry Blossom

1 oz / 3 cl	Cognac
2/3 oz / 2 cl	cherry brandy
1/2 oz / 1.5 cl	maraschino liqueur
1/2 oz / 1.5 cl	orange curaçao
1/2 oz / 1.5 cl	fresh lemon juice
GARNISH	maraschino cherry

Combine the ingredients in a shaker with ice and shake. Strain into a chilled cocktail glass. Add the garnish.

Bookmark

1 2/3 oz / 5 cl	bourbon
1/2 oz / 1.5 cl	vintage Port
1/3 oz / 1 cl	cinnamon syrup (page 20)
2 dashes	Angostura bitters
5	Morello cherries, pitted
GARNISH	twist of orange

Combine the bourbon, syrup, Port, and bitters in a mixing glass and stir while gradually adding ice cubes. Muddle the cherries in the bottom of an old-fashioned glass. Add ice cubes. Strain the contents of the mixing glass into the old-fashioned glass and stir. Add the garnish.

‹ ‹ ‹ **Blueberry Muffin Martini** is enhanced by the novel garnish set across the glass.

Cherry Crush

2 oz / 6 cl	gin
1 oz / 3 cl	maraschino liqueur
1/2 oz / 1.5 cl	fresh lemon juice
4	sweet cherries, pitted
GARNISH	fresh red cherry

Muddle the cherries in the bottom of a shaker. Add remaining ingredients and ice and shake. Double-strain into a chilled cocktail glass. Add the garnish.

Cherry Mash Sour

1½ oz / 4.5 cl	Jack Daniels whiskey
1 oz / 3 cl	Cherry Herring liqueur
1 oz / 3 cl	fresh lemon juice
½ oz / 1.5 cl	simple syrup (page 20)
dash	orange bitters
GARNISH	cherry, orange twist

Combine the ingredients in a shaker with ice and shake. Strain into an old-fashioned glass filled with ice. Add the garnish.

Singapore Sling

1⅓ oz / 4 cl	gin
⅔ oz / 2 cl	cherry brandy
⅓ oz / 1 cl	Bénédictine
⅓ oz / 1 cl	Cointreau
⅓ oz / 1 cl	fresh lemon juice
2⅓ oz / 7 cl	orange juice
2⅓ oz / 7 cl	pineapple juice
GARNISH	wedge of pineapple, fresh red cherry

Combine the ingredients in a shaker with ice and shake. Pour into a highball filled with cubed ice. Put the garnish on the edge of the glass.

‹ ‹ ‹ You can't beat the fullness of flavors in the classic **Singapore Sling**.

coconut

Coconut milk is soft on the mouth and has a fruity,
nutty flavor. For cocktails you can use coconut cream,
coconut milk, or a coconut-flavored spirit such as rum.

Coco Affair (nonalcoholic)

1½ oz / 4.5 cl	coconut cream
1⅓ oz / 4 cl	fresh orange juice
1⅓ oz / 4 cl	pineapple juice
½ oz / 1.5 cl	heavy (double) cream
6	fresh strawberries, diced
GARNISH	half a strawberry

Combine the ingredients in a blender and
blend until smooth. Add a scoop of crushed
ice and blend again. Pour into a highball or a
tumbler. Slit the strawberry and place it on
the rim of the glass. Serve with a straw.

Cococabana

1 oz / 3 cl	coconut rum
1 oz / 3 cl	melon liqueur
3⅓ oz / 10 cl	pineapple juice
1 oz / 3 cl	coconut cream
GARNISH	slice of star fruit

Combine the ingredients in a blender with a
scoop of crushed ice and blend until smooth.
Pour into a goblet. Slit the star fruit and place
it on the rim of the glass. Serve with a straw.

El Coco Mio

2 oz / 6 cl	overproof rum
2 oz / 6 cl	coconut cream
1 oz / 3 cl	fresh lime juice
GARNISH	wedge of pineapple, cherry

Combine the ingredients in a blender with
2 scoops of crushed ice and blend for 10
seconds. Pour into a colada glass and serve
with a straw. Add the garnish.

Piña Colada

1⅔ oz / 5 cl	light rum
3⅓ oz / 10 cl	pineapple juice
1⅔ oz / 5 cl	coconut cream
GARNISH	slice of pineapple, maraschino cherry

Combine the ingredients in a blender and
blend for a few seconds. Add a scoop of
crushed ice and blend for 5 seconds. Pour
into a colada glass or goblet. Put the garnish
on a cocktail stick and place it on the edge of
the glass.

Pirate's Sip

1 oz / 3 cl	coconut rum
1 oz / 3 cl	overproof rum
2 oz / 6 cl	coconut cream
1 oz / 3 cl	fresh lime juice
GARNISH	wedge of pineapple, fresh red cherry

Combine the ingredients in a blender with crushed ice and blend until smooth. Pour into a colada glass. Skewer the cherry and pineapple wedge on a cocktail stick and place the wedge on the rim of the glass.

Saoc Cocktail

2 oz / 6 cl	coconut rum
1 oz / 3 cl	fresh lime juice
½ oz / 1.5 cl	maple syrup
1	egg white
GARNISH	fresh coconut shavings, cinnamon

Combine the ingredients in a shaker with ice and shake. Strain into a chilled cocktail glass. Garnish with the coconut shavings and a sprinkle of cinnamon.

Sensual Bay Breeze

1½ oz / 4.5 cl	coconut rum
2 oz / 6 cl	cranberry juice
2 oz / 6 cl	pineapple juice

Combine the ingredients in a shaker with ice and shake. Strain into a highball filled with ice.

cranberry

Bitter and sour are the basic tastes in cranberries.
Cranberry juice is available as white or red juice and is
good for cutting the sweetness in a cocktail. It is also full
of antioxidants and vitamins, so you can sip a healthy drink.

Cape Cod

2 oz / 6 cl	vodka
4 oz / 12 cl	cranberry juice
GARNISH	wedge of lime

Combine the ingredients in a highball filled
with ice and stir. Add the garnish.

Cosmopolitan

1½ oz / 5 cl	vodka
½ oz / 1.5 cl	Cointreau
½ oz / 1.5 cl	fresh lime juice
1 oz / 3 cl	cranberry juice
GARNISH	twist of orange

Combine the ingredients in a shaker with ice
and shake. Strain into a chilled cocktail glass
and add the garnish if desired.

Cranberry Sauce

1½ oz / 4.5 cl	vodka
½ oz / 1.5 cl	cranberry liqueur
1 oz / 3 cl	cranberry juice
½ oz / 1.5 cl	fresh lime juice
GARNISH	wedge of lime

Combine the ingredients in a shaker with ice
and shake. Strain into a chilled cocktail glass.
Slit the lime and place it on the rim of the
glass.

For an elegant pre-dinner drink, turn to
the modern classic **Cosmopolitan**.❯❯❯

fig

Another seasonal luxury fruit, fresh figs have a delicate, musky flavor when ripe and are best eaten at room temperature. They add sensuality to the flavor of a cocktail. Look for fruit that yields to the touch but is not mushy.

Fickle Fig

1 oz / 3 cl	grappa
dash	grenadine
1 tsp	honey
2	fresh figs, peeled and diced
	Prosecco (Italian sparkling wine)

Lightly muddle the figs in the bottom of a shaker. Add ice and the remaining ingredients except the Prosecco and shake. Strain into a chilled Champagne coupe. Top up with the Prosecco and stir.

Fig Supreme

2 oz / 6 cl	añejo (aged) tequila
½ oz / 1.5 cl	Grand Marnier
½ oz / 1.5 cl	fresh lime juice
dash	grenadine
1	ripe, dark fig, peeled and diced
GARNISH	wedge of fig

Gently muddle the fig with the lime juice and grenadine in the bottom of a shaker. Add ice and the remaining ingredients and shake well. Strain into an old-fashioned glass filled with crushed ice. Slit the fig and place it on the rim of the glass.

Sweet Indulgence

2 oz / 6 cl	reposado tequila
1 tsp	honey
½ oz / 1.5 cl	hot water
1 oz / 3 cl	fresh lime juice
1	fresh fig, peeled and diced
GARNISH	wedge of fig

Muddle the fig with the hot water and honey in the bottom of a shaker. Add ice and the remaining ingredients and shake. Strain into a chilled cocktail glass. Add the garnish.

grapefruit

There are three types of grapefruit flesh: white, pink, and ruby. Each flavor is different but they all are slightly sharp with a hint of sweetness. The fruit is excellent for fresh juice and as a garnish.

Bacardi Grapefruit Blossom

1⅓ oz / 4 cl	Bacardi rum
2 dashes	maraschino liqueur
1⅓ oz / 4 cl	pink grapefruit juice

Combine the ingredients in a shaker with ice and shake. Strain into a chilled cocktail glass.

Bitter Kiss

1 oz / 3 cl	vodka
1 oz / 3 cl	ruby red grapefruit juice
2 dashes	Angostura bitters
	Champagne

Combine the vodka, juice, and bitters in a shaker with ice and shake. Pour into a Champagne flute. Top up with Champagne and stir.

El Palomar

2 oz / 6 cl	Bacardi
½ oz / 1.5 cl	Velvet Falernum liqueur
2 oz / 6 cl	fresh pink grapefruit juice
½ oz / 1.5 cl	fresh lime juice
	club soda or sparkling water

Combine all the ingredients except the soda in a highball. Add crushed or cracked ice and stir well. Then add more ice and top up with the soda or sparkling water.

Morning Margarita

1⅔ oz / 5 cl	tequila
½ oz / 1.5 cl	Cointreau
1 oz / 3 cl	pink grapefruit juice
½ oz / 1.5 cl	fresh lime juice
1 tsp	medium-cut grapefruit marmalade
1 tsp	agave syrup
GARNISH	strips of grapefruit peel

Combine the ingredients in a shaker with ice and shake hard so the flavor of the marmalade is released. Strain into an old-fashioned glass filled with ice. Add the garnish.

Papa Doble

1²⁄₃ oz / 5 cl	rum
¹⁄₃ oz / 1 cl	maraschino liqueur
²⁄₃ oz / 2 cl	fresh white grapefruit juice
¹⁄₃ oz / 1 cl	simple syrup (page 20)
½ oz / 1.5 cl	fresh lime juice
GARNISH	maraschino cherry

Combine the ingredients in a shaker filled with ice and shake. Strain into a chilled cocktail glass. Add the garnish on a cocktail stick.

Sal's Tart

2 oz / 6 cl	vanilla vodka
½ oz / 1.5 cl	fresh lime juice
1 tsp	clear honey
1 oz / 3 cl	pink grapefruit juice
GARNISH	grapefruit spiral

Combine the ingredients in a shaker with ice and shake. Strain into a chilled cocktail glass. Add the garnish.

Salty Dog

1¹⁄₃ oz / 4 cl	vodka
1¹⁄₃ oz / 4 cl	fresh grapefruit juice
	fine sea salt
	wedge of lemon

Use the salt and the wedge of lemon to crust the rim of a cocktail glass (see page 14). Combine the vodka and grapefruit juice in a shaker with ice and shake. Strain into prepared glass.

guava

As exotic as its name, the guava is sweet and tropical,
with a musky fragrance. Guava juice goes well with a lot
of other flavors and is easier to work with than
the fresh fruit, which has a lot of seeds.

Gee Whiz

2 oz / 6 cl	light rum
3 oz / 9 cl	guava juice
2 oz / 6 cl	pineapple juice
1 oz / 3 cl	fresh lime juice
quarter	fresh guava, diced
GARNISH	slice of lime

Combine the ingredients in a blender and
blend until smooth. Pour into a highball filled
with crushed ice. Slit the lime and place it on
the rim of the glass. Serve with a straw.

St. James

1²⁄₃ oz / 5 cl	aged rum
½ oz / 1.5 cl	Campari
2¹⁄₃ oz / 7 cl	guava juice
²⁄₃ oz / 2 cl	fresh lime juice
¹⁄₃ oz / 1 cl	simple syrup (page 20)
GARNISH	wedge of guava, mint, raspberry, 2 blueberries

Combine the ingredients in a shaker with ice
and shake. Strain into a highball filled with
ice. Add the garnish on a cocktail stick on the
edge of the glass.

Velvet Touch

2 oz / 6 cl	light rum
½ oz / 1.5 cl	Grand Marnier
3 oz / 9 cl	guava juice
1 oz / 3 cl	fresh lime juice
1 tsp	clear honey
GARNISH	wedge of lime

Combine the ingredients in a shaker with ice
and shake. Strain into a highball filled with
ice. Slit the lime and place it on the edge of
the glass.

❬ ❬ ❬ **St. James** has a regal appearance
created by the crown of garnish.

lemon

Lemon is a versatile, essential ingredient in cocktails because of its sharp flavor. Its fresh juice balances sweet liqueurs and syrups and adds its own piquancy. For garnishes, use it as a twist, a slice, a spiral, or a wedge, plus you can grate the zest over a drink.

Amalfi Dream

1²⁄₃ oz / 5 cl	vodka
1 oz / 3 cl	limoncello
1 oz / 3 cl	fresh lemon juice
4 or 5	fresh mint leaves
GARNISH	slice of lemon, sprig of mint

Combine the ingredients in a shaker with ice and shake. Strain into an old-fashioned glass filled with ice. Add the garnish.

Lemon Beat

2 oz / 6 cl	cachaça
1 oz / 3 cl	fresh lemon juice
2 tsps	clear honey
GARNISH	lemon slice

Combine the honey and cachaça in a shaker and stir to dissolve the honey. Add ice and the lemon juice and shake. Strain into an old-fashioned glass filled with ice. Slit the lemon slice and place it on the rim of the glass.

Bella Donna

1²⁄₃ oz / 5 cl	light rum
²⁄₃ oz / 2 cl	limoncello
²⁄₃ oz / 2 cl	fresh lemon juice
dash	rose syrup (page 23)
	Champagne
GARNISH	lemon spiral

Combine all the ingredients except the Champagne in a shaker with ice and shake. Strain into a chilled cocktail glass. Add a dash of Champagne on top of the drink and add the garnish.

Lemon Curd Martini

2 oz / 6 cl	lemon vodka
2 tsps	lemon curd
½ oz / 1.5 cl	fresh lemon juice
GARNISH	wedge of lemon

Combine the ingredients in a shaker with ice and shake. Strain into a chilled cocktail glass. Slit the lemon wedge and place it on the rim of the glass.

Amalfi Dream has a fresh citrus fragrance enhanced with mint. ❯ ❯ ❯

Lemon Drop

1½ oz / 4.5 cl	vodka
⅔ oz / 2 cl	fresh lemon juice
1 tsp	simple syrup (page 20)
	superfine (caster) sugar
	wedge of lemon
GARNISH	twist of lemon

Use the sugar and the wedge of lemon to crust the rim of a cocktail glass (page 14). Combine the ingredients in a shaker with ice and shake. Strain into the prepared glass. Add the garnish.

Lemon Gin Collins

1 oz / 3 cl	gin
¾ oz / 2.5 cl	limoncello
⅓ oz / 1 cl	simple syrup (page 20)
½ oz / 1.5 cl	fresh lemon juice
	club soda
GARNISH	wedge of lemon

Combine all the ingredients except the club soda in a shaker with ice and shake. Strain into a highball filled with ice and stir. Top up with club soda and stir. Squeeze the wedge of lemon over the drink and drop it in. Serve with two straws.

Lemon Meringue

1⅔ oz / 5 cl	lemon vodka
½ oz / 1.5 cl	Drambuie
1 oz / 3 cl	fresh lemon juice
dash	simple syrup (page 20)
GARNISH	shredded lemon peel

Combine the ingredients in a shaker with ice and shake. Strain into a chilled cocktail glass. Add the garnish.

Lemon Sherbet

1½ oz / 4.5 cl	reposado tequila
½ oz / 1.5 cl	limoncello
¾ oz / 2.5 cl	fresh lemon juice
2 tsps	vanilla sugar
GARNISH	lemon zest

Combine the ingredients in a shaker with ice and shake. Strain into a chilled cocktail glass. Add the garnish.

Sgroppino al Limone

1 oz / 3 cl	vodka
1 oz / 3 cl	heavy (double) cream
2	scoops lemon sorbet
	Prosecco
GARNISH	grated lemon zest, mint leaf

Combine the vodka, cream, and sorbet in a bowl and whip until the mixture is light and airy. This will take some time. Pour into a Champagne flute and top up with Prosecco. Add the garnish.

Vodka Sour

1²⁄₃ oz / 5 cl	vodka
1 oz / 3 cl	fresh lemon juice
1	pasteurized egg white
½ oz / 1.5 cl	simple syrup (page 20)
GARNISH	maraschino cherry, slice of orange

Combine the ingredients in a shaker with ice and shake. Strain into a cocktail glass. Add the garnish on a cocktail stick.

Whiskey Sour

2 oz / 6 cl	bourbon
1 oz / 3 cl	fresh lemon juice
½ oz / 1.5 cl	simple syrup (page 20)
dash	pasteurized egg white
GARNISH	slice of orange

Combine the ingredients in a shaker with ice and shake. Strain into a cocktail glass. Add the garnish.

Great for any occasion, the **Sgroppino al Limone** is delightfully refreshing. ❯ ❯ ❯

lime

The true flavor of lime is captured in this section of classic recipes. With a more assertive, sharp flavor than lemon, the lime is the key ingredient in a margarita, Mojito (page 132), and Daiquiri.

Caipirinha

1⅔ oz / 5 cl	cachaça
1	small fresh lime
1½ tsps	superfine (caster) sugar

Wash the lime and slice off the top and bottom. Cut the lime into small segments from top to bottom. Muddle the lime and sugar in the bottom of an old-fashioned glass, making sure the sugar dissolves. Add ice and the cachaça and stir well. Serve with a stirrer. A straw is optional.

Daiquiri

1⅔ oz / 5 cl	light rum
1 oz / 3 cl	fresh lime juice
1 tsp	superfine (caster) sugar
GARNISH	wedge of lime

Combine the ingredients in a shaker with ice and shake long and sharp to dissolve the sugar. Strain into a chilled cocktail glass. Add the garnish.

Kamikaze Shooter

⅔ oz / 2 cl	vodka
⅓ oz / 1 cl	Cointreau
⅔ oz / 2 cl	fresh lime juice
	wedge of lime

Combine all ingredients except lime wedge in a shaker with ice and shake. Strain into a shot glass. Serve with a wedge of lime on the side. Take a bite of lime, then drink.

Margarita

1⅓ oz / 4 cl	silver tequila
¾ oz / 2.5 cl	Cointreau
⅔ oz / 2 cl	lime juice
	fine sea salt
	wedge of lime
GARNISH	slice of lime

Use the salt and the wedge of lime to crust half the rim of a chilled cocktail glass (see page 14). Combine the ingredients in a shaker with ice and shake. Strain into the glass. Slit the lime and place it on the rim of the glass.

Pisco Sour

1⅔ oz / 5 cl	pisco (brandy from Chile/Peru)
1 oz / 3 cl	fresh lime juice
1	pasteurized egg white
2 dashes	Angostura bitters
dash	simple syrup (page 20)
GARNISH	wedge of lime

Combine the ingredients in a shaker with ice and shake. Strain into a chilled cocktail glass. Slit the lime and place it on the rim of the glass.

Tommy's Margarita

1⅔ oz / 5 cl	reposado tequila
1 oz / 3 cl	fresh lime juice
1 oz / 3 cl	agave syrup
	fine sea salt
	wedge of lime
GARNISH	wedge of lime

Use the salt and the wedge of lime to crust a chilled cocktail glass (see page 14). Combine the ingredients in a shaker with ice and shake. Strain into the prepared glass. Slit the lime and place it on the rim of the glass.

Vodka Gimlet

1⅔ oz / 5 cl	frozen vodka
⅔ oz / 2 cl	Rose's lime juice
GARNISH	thin wedge of lime

Pour the frozen vodka into an old-fashioned glass filled with ice. Add the lime juice and stir. Slit the lime and place it on the rim of the glass.

lychee

Here is a subtropical fruit with white-pink translucent flesh that's glossy like a grape's. Its flavor is sweet on the tongue with a hint of fragrance. Fresh lychees can be muddled to release flavor.

Chinese Lily

1⅓ oz / 4 cl	tequila
⅔ oz / 2 cl	lychee liqueur
⅔ oz / 2 cl	lychee puree
½ oz / 1.5 cl	fresh lemon juice
dash	orgeat syrup

Combine the ingredients in a shaker with ice and shake. Strain into a chilled cocktail glass.

Lychee Crush

1⅔ oz / 5 cl	golden rum
1 oz / 3 cl	lychee liqueur
½ oz / 1.5 cl	fresh lemon juice
dash	simple syrup (page 20)
half	fresh kiwi fruit
GARNISH	peeled lychee

Muddle the flesh of the kiwi in the bottom of a shaker. Add the remaining ingredients and ice and shake. Double-strain into a chilled cocktail glass. Add the garnish.

Lychee La La

2 oz / 6 cl	gin
½ oz / 2 cl	simple syrup (page 20)
3	lemon wedges
3	lychees
1	lemongrass stem, shredded
GARNISH	lemongrass stem, peeled lychee

Muddle the lychees, lemongrass, and lemon wedges with simple syrup in the bottom of a shaker. Add ice and the gin and shake well. Double-strain into a chilled cocktail glass. Put the garnish on a cocktail stick and place it on the edge of the drink.

Lychee Lover

1⅔ oz / 5 cl	vodka
1 oz / 3 cl	lychee liqueur
⅔ oz / 2 cl	fresh lemon juice
dash	pink grapefruit juice
GARNISH	small orchid

Combine the ingredients in a shaker with ice and shake. Strain into a chilled cocktail glass. Add the garnish resting on the rim.

Lychee Rickey

1½ oz / 4.5 cl	gin
¾ oz / 2.5 cl	lychee liqueur
½ oz / 1.5 cl	fresh lime juice
	club soda

GARNISH wedge of lime

Combine the gin, lychee liqueur, and lime juice in a shaker with ice and shake. Strain into a highball filled with ice and top up with club soda. Add the garnish.

Lychee-tini

1⅔ oz / 5 cl	vodka
½ oz / 1.5 cl	lychee liqueur
⅔ oz / 2 cl	lychee juice, drained from a can of lychees

GARNISH peeled lychee

Combine the ingredients in a shaker with ice and shake. Strain into a chilled cocktail glass. Slit the lychee and place it on the rim of the glass.

North Sea Breeze

2 oz / 6 cl	gin
2⅓ oz / 7 cl	lychee juice, drained from a can of lychees
3 oz / 9 cl	grapefruit juice

GARNISH wedge of lime

Pour the ingredients one at a time into a highball filled with ice. Squeeze the wedge of lime into the drink, then drop it in.

mango

Lush and full of juice, the mango has the flavor of the Caribbean in its essence. The fresh, sweet mango is brilliant for blended cocktails. Rich in antioxidants, it is a glorious fruit.

Frescolina

2 oz / 6 cl	vodka
⅔ oz / 2 cl	Cointreau
½ oz / 1.5 cl	mango puree
⅓ oz / 1 cl	fresh lime juice
GARNISH	wedge of mango

Combine the ingredients in a shaker with ice and shake. Double-strain through a tea strainer into a chilled cocktail glass. Slit the mango and place it on the rim of the glass.

Frozen Mango Daiquiri

1⅔ oz / 5 cl	light rum
½ oz / 1.5 cl	mango liqueur
1 oz / 3 cl	fresh lime juice
quarter	fresh mango, peeled and diced
GARNISH	wedge of mango

Combine the ingredients in a blender with a scoop of crushed ice and blend until smooth. Pour into an old-fashioned glass. Slit the mango and place it on the rim of the glass. Serve with a straw.

Fruity Mimosa *serves 6*

5 oz / 15 cl	fresh orange juice
2 oz / 6 cl	fresh lime juice
1	large mango, peeled and diced
750 ml	Prosecco (Italian sparkling wine)

Combine the mango, orange juice, and lime juice in a blender and blend until smooth. Add a scoop of crushed ice and blend again. Pour the mixture into a large pitcher, then slowly add the Prosecco. Stir. Divide among 6 Champagne flutes.

Last Mango in Paris

1¾ oz / 5 cl	añejo (aged) tequila
dash	absinthe or Pernod
1½ oz / 4.5 cl	mango puree
½ oz / 1.5 cl	fresh lime juice
1 tsp	agave syrup
GARNISH	mango slice

Pour the absinthe or Pernod into a chilled Champagne coupe, swirl it around to coat the glass, and discard any excess. Combine the remaining ingredients in a cocktail shaker with ice and shake. Strain into the prepared glass and add the garnish.

Mango Cosmopolitan

2 oz / 6 cl	Malibu mango rum
½ oz / 1.5 cl	fresh lemon juice
⅓ oz / 1 cl	cranberry juice
GARNISH	twist of lemon

Combine the ingredients in a shaker with ice and shake. Strain into a chilled cocktail glass. Add the garnish.

Mango-lick

¾ oz / 2.5 cl	licorice-infused cachaça
¾ oz / 2.5 cl	mango-infused cachaça
⅓ oz / 1 cl	mango liqueur
1 slice	mango, diced
half	fresh lime, diced

Infuse some cachaça with licorice root for one day; infuse some cachaça with fresh, ripe mango for two days. Muddle the mango and lime in the bottom of a mixing glass. Add crushed ice and the cachaças and mango liqueur. Stir well. Pour into an old-fashioned glass.

Mangorita

1⅓ oz / 4 cl	añejo (aged) tequila
⅔ oz / 2 cl	Grand Marnier
⅔ oz / 2 cl	mango puree
½ oz / 1.5 cl	fresh lime juice
dash	agave syrup
GARNISH	wedge of lime

Combine the ingredients in a shaker with ice and shake. Strain into a chilled cocktail glass. Slit the lime and place it on the rim of the glass.

melon

The flavor depends on the type of melon you use. Cantaloupe, honeydew, and watermelon varieties add superb sweet and juicy flavors to any cocktail and go especially well with ginger and rum.

Cantaloupe Cup

2 oz / 6 cl	light rum
½ oz / 1.5 cl	fresh orange juice
½ oz / 1.5 cl	fresh lime juice
dash	simple syrup (page 20)
half	fresh cantaloupe, seeded and chopped
GARNISH	slice of melon

Combine the ingredients in a blender with a small scoop of crushed ice and blend until smooth. Pour into an old-fashioned glass filled with ice. Add the garnish.

Demon Melon

1⅔ oz / 5 cl	silver tequila
1 oz / 3 cl	simple syrup (page 20)
1 oz / 3 cl	fresh lime juice
¾ cup	diced fresh yellow-fleshed melon
GARNISH	melon balls of different colors

Combine the ingredients in a blender with a small scoop of crushed ice and blend until smooth. Strain into a large goblet filled with ice. Add the garnish.

Gypsy Water

2 oz / 6 cl	light rum
3 cubes	watermelon, frozen
1 oz / 3 cl	freshly pressed watermelon juice
	lime and sugar foam*

Combine the rum, watermelon, and juice in a shaker with ice and shake. Pour into a chilled cocktail glass and top with the lime and sugar foam.

*To make the lime and sugar foam, put 1 sheet of bloomed gelatin, 4 pasteurized egg whites, one-quarter part hot water, one-quarter part sugar syrup, and one-quarter part fresh lime juice in an iSi cream canister. Charge with two CO_2 cartridges and place in the refrigerator before use.

Melon Babe

1²/₃ oz / 5 cl	lemon vodka
²/₃ oz / 2 cl	fresh lemon juice
1 oz / 3 cl	simple syrup (page 20)
½ cup	diced cantaloupe
	mineral water

GARNISH   twist of orange

Combine all the ingredients except the mineral water in a blender with crushed ice and blend until smooth. Pour into a highball filled with ice. Top up with water. Use a lighter or a match to lightly flame the outside of the twist and drop it into the drink.

Melon Ball

1 oz / 3 cl	vodka
1 oz / 3 cl	melon liqueur
3¹/₃ oz / 10 cl	pineapple juice

GARNISH   3 assorted melon balls

Combine the ingredients in a shaker with ice and shake. Strain into a highball filled with ice. Add the garnish on a cocktail stick.

Melon Patch

1²/₃ oz / 5 cl	vodka
1 oz / 3 cl	melon liqueur
½ oz / 1.5 cl	triple sec
	club soda

GARNISH   slice of orange

Combine the vodka, melon liqueur, and triple sec in a shaker with ice and shake. Strain into a highball filled with ice. Top up with club soda. Add the garnish.

Melon-tini

2 oz / 6 cl	vodka
1 oz / 3 cl	honeydew melon juice
1 oz / 3 cl	cantaloupe juice

GARNISH   melon ball

Make juices by blending half of each type of fresh melon and straining the pulp. Combine the ingredients in a shaker with ice and shake. Strain into a cocktail glass. Add the garnish.

olive

Black olives are more bitter than the green variety and range in flavor from mild to vibrant, depending on how they were cured. Green olives, such as the Spanish Manzanilla, are perfect for the classic gin Martini (page 37). They have a light, salty flavor. Whatever the color, be sure to use brine-cured olives for cocktails, not oil-cured.

Dirty Martini

2 oz / 6 cl	vodka
1 oz / 3 cl	green olive brine
dash	dry vermouth
GARNISH	green olives

Combine the ingredients in a mixing glass with ice and stir. Strain into a chilled cocktail glass. Add the garnish on a cocktail stick. To make the drink less dirty, reduce the olive brine.

Personalit-ini

2 oz / 6 cl	vodka
dash	dry vermouth
dash	black olive juice
GARNISH	green olives

Combine the ingredients in a mixing glass with ice and stir until the liquid is cold and frosty. Strain into a chilled cocktail glass. Add the garnish.

Naked New York

2 oz / 6 cl	vodka
⅓ oz / 1 cl	dry vermouth
dash	olive brine
GARNISH	blue cheese–stuffed olives

Combine the ingredients in a mixing glass with ice and stir. Pour into a chilled cocktail glass and add the garnish.

Chilled to perfection, the cocktail glass contains the perfect **Dirty Martini** mix. ❭ ❭ ❭

orange

Oranges come in two basic types: bitter and sweet. The peel of bitter oranges is used to make orange curaçao liqueur. Sweet oranges are used to make fresh juice. Blood oranges are exceptionally sweet and rich in flavor, and their red color brightens a cocktail.

Breakfast Martini

1²⁄₃ oz / 5 cl	gin
½ oz / 1.5 cl	Cointreau
½ oz / 1.5 cl	fresh lemon juice
1 full tsp	thin-cut orange marmalade
GARNISH	shredded orange peel

Combine the ingredients in a shaker with ice and shake. Strain into a chilled cocktail glass. Add the garnish.

Citrus Touch

1¹⁄₃ oz / 4 cl	orange vodka
²⁄₃ oz / 2 cl	Galliano liqueur
3 oz / 7.5 cl	fresh orange juice
½ oz / 1.5 cl	fresh lime juice
¹⁄₃ oz / 1 cl	simple syrup (page 20)
	flesh of 1 fresh passion fruit
	sprig of fresh tarragon
GARNISH	¼ passion fruit, small sprig of tarragon

Combine the ingredients in a shaker with ice and shake hard to break down the tarragon. Double-strain into a highball filled with ice. Add the garnish and serve with a straw.

‹ ‹ ‹ A new classic, **Breakfast Martini**, helped to spread my reputation throughout the world.

Mad Mandarine

1 oz / 3 cl	Mandarine Napoleon liqueur
½ oz / 1.5 cl	chocolate liqueur
1 oz / 3 cl	fresh orange juice
²⁄₃ oz / 2 cl	heavy (double) cream
dash	orange bitters
GARNISH	orange spiral

Combine the ingredients in a shaker with ice and shake. Strain into a chilled cocktail glass. Add the garnish.

Maiden's Prayer

1¹⁄₃ oz / 4 cl	gin
²⁄₃ oz / 2 cl	Cointreau
²⁄₃ oz / 2 cl	fresh orange juice
¹⁄₃ oz / 1 cl	fresh lemon juice
GARNISH	twist of orange

Combine the ingredients in a shaker with ice and shake. Strain into a chilled cocktail glass. Add the garnish.

Metropolis

1⅔ oz / 5 cl	mandarin vodka
⅔ oz / 2 cl	Mandarine Napoleon liqueur
⅔ oz / 2 cl	fresh lemon juice
½ oz / 1.5 cl	simple syrup (page 20)
GARNISH	twist of orange

Combine the ingredients in a shaker with ice and shake. Strain into a chilled cocktail glass. Add the garnish.

Orange Blossom

1½ oz / 4.5 cl	gin
½ oz / 1.5 cl	Cointreau
1½ oz / 4.5 cl	fresh orange juice
GARNISH	orange peel

Combine the ingredients in a shaker with ice and shake. Strain into a chilled cocktail glass. Add the garnish.

Orange-tini

2 oz / 6 cl	gin
½ oz / 1.5 cl	Cointreau
⅓ oz / 1 cl	dry vermouth
2 dashes	orange bitters
GARNISH	twist of orange

Combine the ingredients in a mixing glass filled with ice and stir. Strain into a chilled cocktail glass. Add the garnish.

Pisco Naranja

1⅔ oz / 5 cl	pisco brandy
½ oz / 1.5 cl	Grand Marnier
2 oz / 6 cl	fresh orange juice
½	egg white
GARNISH	wedge of orange

Combine the ingredients in a shaker with ice and shake. Strain into an old-fashioned glass filled with ice and add the garnish.

Santiago

1½ oz / 4.5 cl	light rum
1½ oz / 4.5 cl	fresh orange juice
⅓ oz / 1 cl	grenadine syrup (page 21)

Combine the ingredients in a shaker with ice and shake. Double-strain into a chilled cocktail glass.

Screwdriver

1¾ oz / 5 cl	vodka
5 oz / 15 cl	fresh orange juice
GARNISH	slice of orange

Pour the vodka into a highball filled with ice. Add the orange juice. Stir well. Add the garnish. Serve with a stirrer.

Tawny Orange Jelly Sour

1²⁄₃ oz / 5 cl	Hendrick's gin
½ oz / 1 cl	honey syrup (page 22)
2 tsps	thick-cut orange marmalade
²⁄₃ oz / 2 cl	fresh lemon juice

GARNISH orange peel, orange spiral

Combine the ingredients in a shaker with ice and shake. Strain through a tea strainer into a chilled Champagne coupe. Drop the orange peel into the drink and place the orange spiral on the rim.

Tequila Sunrise

1²⁄₃ oz / 5 cl	tequila
5 oz / 15 cl	fresh orange juice
2 dashes	grenadine

GARNISH orange spiral

Pour the tequila and orange juice into a highball filled with ice. Stir. Splash in the grenadine and watch it sink down through the drink. Add the garnish. Serve with a straw.

Filled with fresh, citrusy, herbal, and peppery flavors, **Citrus Touch** offers intrigue. ❯ ❯ ❯

papaya

The papaya was originally cultivated in Mexico but is now grown in most tropical countries. This beloved and very nutritious tropical fruit was reputedly called "the fruit of the angels" by Christopher Columbus. Papayas were brought to the United States in the twentieth century and are cultivated in Hawaii, the major U.S. producer since the 1920s. The Hawaiian fruit is smaller and sweeter than other varieties. You should be able to press your thumb into a ripe fruit, but if it is very soft or has a sweet smell, it is overripe. Adding lime to papaya magically brings the flavor of this fruit to life.

Avion Papaya Smash *serves 2*

2 oz / 6 cl	golden rum
1 oz / 3 cl	Aperol
1 oz / 3 cl	agave syrup
1 oz / 3 cl	fresh orange juice
1 oz / 3 cl	fresh lime juice
	flesh of ½ fresh papaya
GARNISH	2 papaya wedges

Muddle the papaya in the bottom of a shaker. Add ice and the remaining ingredients and shake. Double-strain into 2 chilled cocktail glasses. Slit the papaya wedges and place them on the rim of each glass.

Batida Papaya

2 oz / 6 cl	cachaça
1 oz / 3 cl	fresh lime juice
¼	fresh papaya
2 tsps	superfine (caster) sugar
GARNISH	papaya wedge

Combine the ingredients in a blender with crushed ice and blend until smooth. Pour into an old-fashioned glass and add the garnish.

Papaya Mexicana

1¾ oz / 5 cl	reposado tequila
¾ oz / 2.5 cl	fresh lime juice
½ oz / 1.5 cl	coconut syrup (page 21)
1¾ oz / 5 cl	unfiltered apple juice
½	medium papaya
GARNISH	papaya slice

Scoop the flesh and seeds of the papaya into a blender. Add the remaining ingredients and blend without ice for about 30 seconds, until smooth. Half-fill a highball with crushed ice and pour the drink over the ice. Add the garnish.

passion fruit

At first taste, you think your mouth has exploded
with sharp acidity, and then the sweet, intense, tropical fruit
comes through. This is a dominant flavor in any cocktail.
Strain out the small black seeds if you prefer.

Bonito

1⅔ oz / 5 cl	tequila
½ oz / 1.5 cl	Grand Marnier
⅓ oz / 1 cl	fresh lime juice
3 oz / 9 cl	passion fruit juice
2 tsps	brown sugar
3	orange wedges
GARNISH	half a passion fruit

Muddle the orange wedges with the sugar
in the bottom of a shaker. Add ice and the
remaining ingredients and shake well. Strain
into a highball filled with crushed ice. Add the
garnish. Serve with a straw.

Deep Passion

1⅓ oz / 4 cl	vodka
½ oz / 1.5 cl	Grand Marnier
3 oz / 9 cl	passion fruit juice
1 oz / 3 cl	fresh lime juice
1	passion fruit
GARNISH	cape gooseberry

Cut passion fruit in half, and scoop the flesh
into a shaker. Add ice and the remaining
ingredients and shake. Strain into a highball
filled with ice. Slit the cape gooseberry and
place it on the rim of the glass.

Passion Fruit Collins

1⅔ oz / 5 cl	vodka or gin
¾ oz / 2.5 cl	fresh lemon juice
2 tsps	simple syrup (page 20)
	pulp of 1 fresh passion fruit
	club soda
GARNISH	passion flower, a few mint leaves

Half-fill an old-fashioned glass with crushed
ice. Add all the ingredients except the club
soda and stir. Top up with more ice and then
the club soda. Add the garnish.

Passion Latina

2 oz / 6 cl	light rum
1 oz / 3 cl	passion fruit puree
1½ tsps	pineapple syrup (page 23)
½ oz / 1.5 cl	fresh lime juice
	pulp of ½ fresh passion fruit
GARNISH	half passion fruit, sprig of mint

Combine the ingredients in a shaker with ice
and shake. Strain into an old-fashioned glass
filled with ice, allowing some of the pulp to
come through. Add the garnish.

peach

The flesh of a white peach has a finer flavor than
the pale yellow variety and is perfect for the classic cocktail,
the Bellini. Sweet, fragrant peach flavor is good combined
with raspberries, vanilla, wine, and cream.

Bellini

1½ oz / 4.5 cl	white peach puree
	Prosecco (Italian sparkling wine)

Pour the peach puree into a chilled
Champagne flute. Top up with Prosecco
and stir gently.

Décollage

1⅔ oz / 5 cl	light rum
¾ oz / 2.5 cl	peach liqueur
1 oz / 3 cl	fresh lemon juice
½ oz / 1.5 cl	simple syrup (page 20)
3 dashes	peach bitters
	club soda
GARNISH	peach wedge

Combine all the ingredients except the club
soda in a shaker with ice and shake. Strain
into a highball filled with ice and top up with
club soda. Add the garnish.

Peach Blossom

1⅓ oz / 4 cl	vodka
⅓ oz / 1 cl	Peche de Vigne
⅔ oz / 2 cl	peach puree
⅓ oz / 1 cl	fresh lemon juice
2	cardamom pods

Muddle the cardamom pods in the bottom of
a shaker. Add ice and the remaining ingredients and shake. Strain into a chilled cocktail
glass.

‹ ‹ ‹ **Peach Blossom**, seen here with
Champagne & Pear Drop, has a
layer of cardamom flavor.

pear

Buttery, creamy flesh defines the best in a pear. Its sweet flavor comes out when the pear is ripe and juicy. Look for skins that are not bruised. An intense pear flavor is good with nutty and spicy ingredients.

Autumn Pear

¾ oz / 2.5 cl	pear vodka
¾ oz / 2.5 cl	Poire Williams liqueur
⅓ oz / 1 cl	limoncello
¾ oz / 2.5 cl	passion fruit juice
dash	lemon juice
dash	simple syrup (page 20)

GARNISH pear wedge

Combine the ingredients in a shaker with ice and shake. Strain into a chilled cocktail glass. Slit the pear wedge and place it on the rim of the glass.

Dolce Pera

1 oz / 3 cl	pear vodka
⅓ oz / 1 cl	fresh lemon juice
1 tsp	superfine (caster) sugar
⅔ oz / 2 cl	pear puree
	Prosecco (Italian sparkling wine)

GARNISH crystallized ginger

Combine all the ingredients except the Prosecco in a shaker with ice and shake. Strain into a Champagne flute. Top up with Prosecco and stir. Add the garnish.

Champagne & Pear Drop

½ oz / 1.5 cl	Cognac
⅓ oz / 1 cl	Passoa liqueur
⅓ oz / 1 cl	pear puree
⅓ oz / 1 cl	chamomile syrup (page 20)
	Champagne

GARNISH stem of red currants

Combine all the ingredients except the Champagne in a shaker with ice and shake. Strain into a chilled Champagne flute. Top up with Champagne and stir. Add the garnish on the rim.

La Poire d'Amour

½ oz / 1.5 cl	Xante pear liqueur
¾ oz / 2.5 cl	Courvoisier
¾ oz / 2.5 cl	pear puree
dash	vanilla syrup (page 24)
dash	cherry bitters
½	ripe pear
4	cardamom pods
	Champagne
	vanilla sugar
	wedge of lemon
GARNISH	slice of pear

Use the vanilla sugar and the wedge of lemon to crust a Champagne coupe (see page 14). Muddle the pear and the cardamom in the bottom of a shaker. Add the remaining ingredients except the Champagne and shake. Strain into the prepared glass. Top up with Champagne and stir. Slit the pear and place it on the rim of the glass.

Pearadise Martini

1⅔ oz / 5 cl	gin
⅔ oz / 2 cl	pear liqueur
1 oz / 3 cl	pear puree
dash	fresh lemon juice
GARNISH	slice of pear

Combine the ingredients in a shaker with ice and shake. Strain into a chilled cocktail glass. Slit the pear slice and place it on the rim of the glass.

Pear-tini

1⅔ oz / 5 cl	vodka
⅓ oz / 1 cl	amaretto
⅓ oz / 1 cl	simple syrup (page 20)
⅔ oz / 2 cl	fresh lemon juice
GARNISH	fan of pear slices (see page 15)

Combine the ingredients in a shaker with ice and shake. Strain into a chilled cocktail glass. Add the garnish.

Woody au Pear

1⅓ oz / 4 cl	bourbon
¾ oz / 2.5 cl	Poire Williams
1¾ oz / 5 cl	pear puree
GARNISH	pear spiral, cinnamon stick

Combine all the ingredients in a shaker with ice and shake. Strain into an old-fashioned glass filled with ice. Add the garnish.

pineapple

With sweet, juicy, and fragrant flesh under a hard and prickly skin,
the rough-leafed varieties are small and have deep-gold flesh,
which is better for juice than the less-sweet, larger varieties.

El Cerro

1¾ oz / 2.5 cl	light rum
1¾ oz / 2.5 cl	dark rum
½ oz / 1.5 cl	orange curaçao
½ oz / 1.5 cl	Galliano liqueur
1⅓ oz / 4 cl	pineapple juice
dash	grenadine
	superfine (caster) sugar
	wedge of lemon
GARNISH	dried pineapple slice, star anise, mint leaf

Combine all the ingredients except the grenadine in a shaker with ice and shake. Strain into a highball filled with crushed ice. Pour the grenadine over the top. Add the garnish.

French Martini

1⅓ oz / 4 cl	vodka
⅔ oz / 2 cl	Chambord liqueur
1 oz / 3 cl	fresh pineapple juice
GARNISH	twist of orange

Combine the ingredients in a shaker with ice and shake. Strain into a chilled cocktail glass and add the garnish.

Mary Pickford

1½ oz / 4 cl	white rum
6 drops	maraschino liqueur
1½ oz / 4 cl	fresh pineapple juice
1 tsp	grenadine
GARNISH	maraschino cherry

Combine the ingredients in a shaker with ice and shake. Strain into a chilled cocktail glass and add the garnish.

Pineapple Dream

1⅔ oz / 5 cl	vodka
⅓ oz / 1 cl	simple syrup (page 20)
⅔ oz / 2 cl	fresh lime juice
½ slice	fresh pineapple, diced
GARNISH	small wedge of pineapple

Muddle the pineapple, syrup, and lime juice in the bottom of a shaker. Add ice and the vodka and shake. Double-strain into an old-fashioned glass filled with ice. Add the garnish. Serve with a straw.

Pineapple Margarita

2 oz / 6 cl	añejo (aged) tequila
½ oz / 1.5 cl	fresh lime juice
dash	agave syrup
½ slice	fresh pineapple, diced
GARNISH	pineapple leaf

Muddle the pineapple with the syrup in the bottom of a shaker. Add ice and the remaining ingredients and shake. Double-strain into a chilled cocktail glass. Slit the pineapple leaf and place it on the rim of the glass.

Playboy II

1²⁄₃ oz / 5 cl	aged rum
½ oz / 1.5 cl	cherry liqueur
1 oz / 3 cl	pineapple juice
dash	fresh lime juice
GARNISH	small orchid

Combine the ingredients in a shaker with ice and shake. Strain into a chilled cocktail glass. Add the flower to the glass, and your telephone number on a cocktail coaster.

Snow White

1²⁄₃ oz / 5 cl	light rum
⅓ oz / 1 cl	simple syrup (page 20)
1 oz / 3 cl	fresh lime juice
1	egg white
½ slice	fresh pineapple

Muddle the pineapple in the bottom of a shaker. Add ice and the remaining ingredients and shake. Double-strain into a chilled cocktail glass.

El Cerro, a Caribbean carnival in a glass. ❯ ❯ ❯

plum

The best known of all the plum brandies is slivovitz, which is made from the small blue sliva (damson) plum common throughout Eastern Europe and the Balkans. Sloe gin is a liqueur flavored with sloe berries, which are related to plums.

Baby Fingers

1 oz / 3 cl	sloe gin
1⅔ oz / 5 cl	gin
2 dashes	Angostura bitters

Combine the ingredients in a shaker with ice and shake. Strain into a chilled cocktail glass.

Blackthorn

1 oz / 3 cl	sweet vermouth
1½ oz / 4.5 cl	sloe gin
GARNISH	twist 0of lemon

Combine the ingredients in a mixing glass with ice and stir. Strain into a chilled cocktail glass. Add the garnish.

Brave Love

2 oz / 6 cl	sloe gin
dash	fresh lemon juice
dash	raspberry juice
1	pasteurized egg white

Combine the ingredients in a shaker with ice and shake. Strain into a chilled cocktail glass.

Dark Side

1½ oz / 4.5 cl	añejo (aged) tequila
½ oz / 1.5 cl	Grand Marnier
1 oz / 3 cl	fresh lime juice
1	peeled dark plum

Muddle the plum in the bottom of a shaker. Add ice and the remaining ingredients and shake. Strain into a chilled cocktail glass.

Deep Plum

1½ oz / 4.5 cl	plum brandy
dash	maraschino liqueur
½ oz / 1.5 cl	fresh lemon juice
½ oz / 1.5 cl	orange juice

Combine the ingredients in a shaker with ice and shake. Strain into a chilled cocktail glass.

Plum Martini

2 oz / 6 cl	vodka
½ oz / 1.5 cl	French dry vermouth
1 tsp	simple syrup (page 20)
1	fresh plum, peeled, pitted, and chopped
GARNISH	wedge of plum

Muddle the plum in the bottom of a shaker. Add ice and the remaining ingredients and shake. Double-strain into a chilled cocktail glass. Slit the wedge of plum and place it on the rim of the glass.

Plum Sour

1½ oz / 4.5 cl	sloe gin
1 oz / 3 cl	fresh lemon juice
½ oz / 1.5 cl	simple syrup (page 20)
1	egg white
1	fresh plum, peeled, pitted, and chopped
GARNISH	wedge of plum

Muddle the plum in the bottom of a shaker. Add ice and the remaining ingredients and shake. Double-strain into an old-fashioned glass filled with ice. Add the garnish.

Sloe Gin Fizz

1⅔ oz / 5 cl	sloe gin
⅓ oz / 1 cl	fresh lemon juice
dash	simple syrup (page 20)
	club soda
GARNISH	slice of lime

Combine all the ingredients except the club soda into a shaker with ice and shake. Strain into a highball and top up with soda. Add the garnish. Serve with a stirrer.

pomegranate

To make fresh pomegranate juice, you need to muddle the seeds, but the effect produces balance of sweet and tart flavors. A few top-quality brands of juice on page 191 will save you the trouble.

Demon Martini

1²⁄₃ oz / 5 cl	gin
½ oz / 1.5 cl	white Lillet
quarter	fresh pomegranate
2	thin slices of sweet chile
	superfine (caster) sugar
	wedge of lemon
GARNISH	thin slice of chile

Use the sugar and the wedge of lemon to crust half of the rim of a chilled cocktail glass (see page 14). Muddle the pomegranate in the bottom of a shaker. Add ice and the remaining ingredients and shake. Strain into the glass. Slit the slice of chile and place it on the rim of the glass, if desired.

Pomegranate Bellini

⅓ oz / 1 cl	Cointreau
	juice of ½ pomegranate
	Prosecco

Combine the Cointreau and pomegranate juice in a shaker with ice and shake. Strain into a Champagne flute and top up with Prosecco.

Pomegranate Julep

1²⁄₃ oz / 5 cl	vodka
1 oz / 3 cl	pomegranate juice
1 oz / 3 cl	grapefruit juice
½ oz / 1.5 cl	honey syrup (page 22)
4	mint leaves
GARNISH	sprig of mint

Muddle the mint with the honey syrup in the bottom of a shaker. Add the remaining ingredients and shake. Strain into an old-fashioned glass filled with ice. Add the garnish.

Pomegranate Margarita

1½ oz / 4.5 cl	reposado tequila
2 tsps	Cointreau
½ oz / 1.5 cl	fresh lime juice
1 tsp	grenadine
	juice of 1 pomegranate
	rock salt
	granulated sugar
	wedge of lime

Crush equal quantities of rock salt and granulated sugar and place the mixture in a small plate. Use the salt-sugar mixture and the wedge of lime to crust half the rim of a chilled cocktail glass (see page 14). Combine the ingredients in a shaker with ice and shake. Strain into the prepared glass.

A **Demon Martini** fills the mouth with pomegranate flavor. ❯ ❯ ❯

Pomegranate Martini

1²⁄₃ oz / 5 cl	vodka
¹⁄₃ oz / 1 cl	maraschino liqueur
½	fresh pomegranate
GARNISH	pomegranate seeds

Squeeze the juice from the pomegranate and reserve a few seeds as garnish. Combine the ingredients in a shaker with ice and shake. Strain into a chilled cocktail glass and add the garnish.

Pomegranny

1³⁄₄ oz / 5 cl	gin
1³⁄₄ oz / 5 cl	pomegranate juice
4 oz / 12 cl	bitter lemon
GARNISH	pomegranate seeds

Pour the ingredients over ice in a highball. Stir and sit a few pomegranate seeds on top of the drink. Serve with a straw.

Pomegrita *serves 6*

6 oz / 18 cl	gin
6	pomegranates
4 tbsps	superfine (caster) sugar

Muddle the pomegranates in the bottom of a shaker and pass the juice through a strainer. Combine the juice, gin, and sugar in a bowl and stir to dissolve the sugar. Freeze the bowl overnight. When ready to serve, use a spoon to break up the mixture. Divide it between 6 shot glasses. Serve with a small teaspoon on the side.

Pome-tini

1²⁄₃ oz / 5 cl	vodka
1 oz / 3 cl	pomegranate juice
½ oz / 1.5 cl	fresh lime juice
½ oz / 1.5 cl	simple syrup (page 20)
GARNISH	orange spiral

Combine the ingredients in a shaker with ice and shake. Strain into a chilled cocktail glass. Add the garnish over the rim of the glass.

Pomiri

1²⁄₃ oz / 5 cl	light rum
½ oz / 1.5 cl	maraschino liqueur
1 oz / 3 cl	pomegranate juice
1 oz / 3 cl	fresh lime juice
½ oz / 1.5 cl	simple syrup (page 20)
GARNISH	wedge of lime

Combine the ingredients in a shaker with ice and shake. Strain into an old-fashioned glass filled with ice. Add the garnish.

‹‹‹ **Red Earl** combines fresh berry flavors with sweetness and a ginger aftertaste.

raspberry

Tart flavors dominate in a fresh red raspberry, so it's best to use raspberry juice with other flavors that aren't sour, such as chocolate, vanilla, rose water, and lavender. Crème de framboise with fresh raspberries is a luxurious combination.

Raspberry Collins

1²⁄₃ oz / 5 cl	raspberry vodka
½ oz / 1.5 cl	Chambord liqueur
½ oz / 1.5 cl	fresh lemon juice
⅓ oz / 1 cl	simple syrup (page 20)
7	fresh raspberries
	club soda
GARNISH	2 raspberries

Muddle the raspberries with the simple syrup in the bottom of a shaker. Add ice and the remaining ingredients except the club soda. Shake well. Strain into a highball filled with ice. Top up with soda and stir. Add the garnish.

Raspberry Torte

1²⁄₃ oz / 5 cl	reposado tequila
⅔ oz / 2 cl	Grand Marnier
⅔ oz	fresh lime juice
1²⁄₃ oz / 5 cl	raspberry puree
dash	orange bitters
GARNISH	raspberry

Combine all the ingredients except the raspberry puree in a blender with 2 scoops of crushed ice and blend for 20 seconds. Pour half the mixture into a Champagne coupe.

Gently layer the raspberry puree over the surface of the drink to create a thin red layer. Top with the mixture remaining in the shaker. Add the garnish to the center of the drink. Serve with a straw.

Red Earl

1½ oz / 4.5 cl	vodka
⅔ oz / 2 cl	limoncello
⅔ oz / 2 cl	raspberry puree
2	raspberries
2	thin slices of fresh ginger
GARNISH	slice of fresh ginger, mint leaf

Muddle the ginger in the bottom of a shaker. Add ice and the remaining ingredients and shake. Double-strain into a chilled cocktail glass. Add the garnish.

Offering spectacular color and creamy texture, **Russian Heart** is a celebration at any time. ❯ ❯ ❯

Russian Heart

1²⁄₃ oz / 5 cl	raspberry vodka
1²⁄₃ oz / 5 cl	fresh red grapefruit juice
½ oz / 1.5 cl	fresh lemon juice
⅓ oz / 1 cl	simple syrup (page 20)
5	raspberries
½	egg white
GARNISH	2 raspberries, sprig of mint

Combine the ingredients in a shaker with ice and shake hard to break down the berries. Strain into an old-fashioned glass filled with ice, allowing some of the berry pulp into the glass. Add the garnish on a cocktail stick on the rim of the glass.

strawberry

A flavor burst enters the mouth with the bite of a fresh, ripe, sweet strawberry. A summer fruit (although you can buy them year-round), the strawberry has a subtle fragrance. Crème de fraise is slightly thicker than regular strawberry liqueur.

Brazilian Lover

1²⁄₃ oz / 5 cl	cachaça
¾ oz / 2.5 cl	crème de fraise
1 oz / 3 cl	fresh lime juice
4	strawberries
2 tsps	dark brown sugar
GARNISH	strawberry fan (page 15), mint tip

Muddle the strawberries in the bottom of a shaker. Add ice and the remaining ingredients and shake. Double-strain into an old-fashioned glass filled with crushed ice. Add the garnish.

Coccinella

1½ oz / 4.5 cl	light rum
⅓ oz / 1 cl	Xante pear liqueur
1 oz / 3 cl	fresh lime juice
⅓ oz / 1 cl	vanilla syrup (page 24)
1	egg white
3 or 4	strawberries
GARNISH	thin slice of strawberry

Lightly muddle the strawberries in the bottom of a shaker. Add ice and the remaining ingredients and shake. Double-strain into a chilled Champagne coupe. Add the garnish.

Franklin Cobbler

1²⁄₃ oz / 5 cl	bourbon
⅔ oz / 2 cl	crème de fraise
dash	simple syrup (page 20)
quarter	slice of orange
2	mint leaves
2	strawberries
GARNISH	quarter slice of orange, mint tip, half strawberry

Gently muddle the orange, mint, and strawberries in the bottom of a large old-fashioned glass. Add the remaining ingredients and fill the glass with crushed ice. Stir vigorously. Add the garnish.

Strawberry Frozen Daiquiri

1²⁄₃ oz / 5 cl	light rum
1 oz / 3 cl	fresh lime juice
½ oz / 1.5 cl	simple syrup (page 20)
4 or 5	strawberries
GARNISH	strawberry fan (page 15)

Combine the ingredients in a blender with 2 scoops of crushed ice and blend until smooth. Pour into a chilled Champagne coupe. Add the garnish.

An unusual twist on a cobbler, **Franklin Cobbler** has a hint of fresh strawberry. 〉〉〉

Strawberry Margarita

1⅔ oz / 5 cl	silver tequila
½ oz / 1.5 cl	strawberry liqueur
½ oz / 1.5 cl	fresh lime juice
handful	strawberries

GARNISH   strawberry, sprig of mint

Combine the ingredients in a blender with crushed ice and blend until smooth. Pour into a Champagne coupe. Add the garnish.

Strawberry Spice

2 oz / 6 cl	cachaça
1 tsp	superfine (caster) sugar
2 dashes	ground cinnamon
3	strawberries, diced

GARNISH   cinnamon stick, slice of strawberry

Muddle the strawberries, sugar, and cinnamon in the bottom of a shaker. Add ice and the cachaça and shake. Strain into an old-fashioned glass filled with ice. Add the garnish.

Tropical Butterfly

1⅔ oz / 5 cl	gin
⅓ oz / 1 cl	elderflower cordial
1⅔ oz / 5 cl	passion fruit juice
½ oz / 1.5 cl	pear puree
3 or 4	fresh strawberries

GARNISH   strawberry

Muddle the strawberries in the bottom of a shaker. Add ice and the remaining ingredients and shake. Strain into a highball filled with ice. Slit the strawberry and place it on the rim of the glass. Serve with straws.

‹ ‹ ‹ **Tropical Butterfly**, with a sweet strawberry aroma, is delightfully refreshing.

tomato

Sweetly acidic tomato flavors abound in farmers' market produce. Look for plump tomatoes with shiny skin. When making tomato juice, strain the juiced pulp through a piece of muslin to remove the seeds.

Bloody Bull

1²⁄₃ oz / 5 cl	vodka
2 oz / 6 cl	beef bouillon or condensed consommé
2 oz / 6 cl	tomato juice
dash	fresh lemon juice
2 dashes	Worcestershire sauce
pinch	celery salt

Combine the ingredients in a shaker with ice and shake. Strain into a highball filled with ice.

Bloody Mary

1²⁄₃ oz / 5 cl	vodka
5 oz / 15 cl	tomato juice
²⁄₃ oz / 2 cl	fresh lemon juice
2 dashes	Worcestershire sauce
2 dashes	Tabasco sauce
pinch	celery salt
pinch	ground black pepper
GARNISH	wedge of lime, celery stalk (optional)

Fill a highball with ice cubes. Pour the tomato and lemon juices into the glass and then add the vodka. Stir. Add the remaining ingredients and stir. Slit the lime and place it on the rim of the glass. Add a stalk of celery if desired. Serve with a stirrer.

Vampiro

1²⁄₃ oz / 5 cl	silver tequila
2¹⁄₃ oz / 7 cl	tomato juice
³⁄₄ oz / 2.5 cl	fresh orange juice
1 tsp	clear honey
¹⁄₃ oz / 1 cl	fresh lime juice
few dashes	Worcestershire sauce
half slice	onion, finely chopped
few slices	hot red chile
pinch	salt
GARNISH	wedge of lime, slice of red chile

Combine the ingredients in a shaker with ice and shake. Strain into a highball filled with ice. Slit the lime and place it on the rim of the glass with the red chile adjacent to it.

Virgin Mary *(nonalcoholic)*

3¹⁄₃ oz / 10 cl	tomato juice
²⁄₃ oz / 2 cl	fresh lemon juice
2 dashes	Worcestershire sauce
dash	Tabasco sauce
pinch	celery salt
GARNISH	wedge of lime, freshly ground black pepper

Combine the ingredients in a highball filled with ice and stir. Add the garnish. Grind pepper over the drink.

watermelon

This large green-skinned fruit, known for its delightful color and flavor, has a sweet taste and a watery juice that lends itself to cocktail recipes.

Vanilla Melon Fizz

1½ oz / 4.5 cl	vodka
¾ oz / 2.5 cl	Galliano liqueur
⅔ oz / 2 cl	fresh lemon juice
dash	simple syrup (page 20)
1 tsp	vanilla sugar
1 tsp	fresh grated coconut
½ cup	diced watermelon

Muddle the watermelon and coconut with the sugar in the bottom of a shaker. Add ice and remaining ingredients and shake. Double-strain into an old-fashioned glass filled with ice.

Watermelon Sombrero

1⅔ oz / 5 cl	silver tequila
½ oz / 1.5 cl	Cointreau
½ oz / 1.5 cl	fresh lime juice
½ oz / 1.5 cl	agave syrup
¾ cup	diced watermelon
GARNISH	small wedge of watermelon

Muddle the watermelon in the bottom of a shaker. Add ice and remaining ingredients and shake. Double-strain into a chilled cocktail glass. Slit the watermelon wedge and place it on the rim of the glass.

Watermelon Martini

2 oz / 6 cl	vodka
dash	simple syrup (page 20)
½ cup	diced watermelon
GARNISH	small wedge of watermelon

Muddle the watermelon in the bottom of a shaker. Add ice and remaining ingredients and shake. Double-strain into a cocktail glass. Slit the watermelon wedge and place it on the rim of the glass.

Watermelon Martini is a refreshing take on the classic Martini-style cocktail. ❯ ❯ ❯

herbs & flowers

Part of the joy of using herbs in cocktails lies in the possibilities of infusion. When you muddle herbs in the bottom of a shaker, you're creating a brief infusion, but if you infuse herbs in spirits for weeks, you can achieve depths of flavor that are much more intense. You can buy ready-made vodkas, rums, and other spirits in many flavors, such as vanilla, cinnamon, and citrus, but the same flavored spirits can be made with a homemade infusion and will taste entirely different, especially when you have managed to get the process down to a fine art.

All infused spirits and liqueurs are produced using the same basic method: an ingredient is steeped in alcohol for a length of time, during which the flavor of the ingredient is diffused in the spirit.

Herbal infusions can be made at home or in the professional bar. All you need is the essential part of a fresh herb, a bottle of the selected spirit, a cool, dark cupboard space, and patience. You can also create schnapps using plum, pear, cherry, apricot, and orange peel, to name but a few of the fruits capable of bringing rich flavor to a spirit. As a sweetener for some liqueurs, you can use homemade simple syrup. Any alcohol can be infused, including vodka, brandy, tequila, and rum.

The combinations of spirit and flavoring are endless, as is the depth of flavor you can achieve. Start by steeping the ingredients for about one week. If, at the end of the week, you find the flavor not as strong as you wanted, leave the mixture for a week or two more. On the other hand, if the flavor is too strong, then add more spirit until the infusion is the strength you like. The amount of flavoring to use is, likewise, up to you. Experiment to please your own taste. Unlike a manufactured infused spirit that lasts indefinitely, a homemade infusion will keep for about six months if stored in a cool, dry place. After that, it will start to lose its freshness.

Bartenders around the globe are making their own unique infusions, using stems of rosemary and lavender, leaves of basil and sage, entire chiles, cinnamon sticks, delicate petals from a rose or two, the rind of citrus fruits . . . all in search of unique flavor.

When you use herbs in cocktails, you will be surprised at the unexpected layers of flavor in the drink. Good luck!

aniseed

The distinctive flavor of aniseed comes from the seeds formed in the flowers of the anise plant, which is similar to licorice, fennel, and tarragon, and was traditionally used to soothe the digestion. Aniseed-flavored liqueurs blend very well with a variety of ingredients, and with the addition of water will become cloudy and creamy.

Absinthe Suissesse

1 oz / 3 cl	absinthe
⅓ oz / 1 cl	anisette
½ oz / 1.5 cl	crème de menthe
dash	orange flower water
1	egg white

Combine the ingredients in a shaker with ice and shake. Strain into a chilled Champagne coupe.

Ecstasy Martini

2 oz / 6 cl	frozen vodka
½ oz / 1.5 cl	Cointreau
½ oz / 1.5 cl	absinthe
1	sugar cube

Combine the vodka and Cointreau in a chilled cocktail glass and stir. Float the absinthe on top and soak the sugar cube in a few drops of absinthe on a bar spoon. Hold the cube over the drink and use a lighter or match to ignite it, holding it close enough to ignite the absinthe on top of the drink. When the sugar is caramelized, drop the cube into the glass. Be very careful, as flames will develop. Wait a few seconds to allow the alcohol to evaporate, then extinguish the flames and stir.

Green Fairy

1½ oz / 4.5 cl	absinthe
1 oz / 3 cl	fresh lemon juice
½ oz / 1.5 cl	chilled water
½ oz / 1.5 cl	simple syrup (page 20)
dash	Angostura bitters
½	egg white

Combine the ingredients in a shaker with ice and shake. Strain into a chilled sherry glass or small goblet.

London Fog

1 oz / 3 cl	gin
1 oz / 3 cl	Pernod
2 oz / 6 cl	water

GARNISH   twist of lemon

Combine the ingredients in an old-fashioned glass. Add ice and stir. Add the garnish.

Spaceman

1½ oz / 4.5 cl	vodka
½ oz / 1.5 cl	dry vermouth
1½ oz / 1.5 cl	Pernod
	dash of grenadine

Combine the ingredients in a mixing glass with ice and stir. Strain into a chilled cocktail glass.

The Morning Mashie

1 oz / 3 cl	gin
½ oz / 1.5 cl	anisette
⅓ oz / 1 cl	Pernod
dash	Angostura bitters
1½ oz / 1.5 cl	fresh lemon juice
½	egg white

Combine the ingredients in a shaker with ice and shake. Strain into a small goblet.

T.N.T.

1 oz / 3 cl	rye whiskey
1 oz / 3 cl	Pernod

GARNISH   twist of orange

Combine the ingredients in a shaker with ice and shake well to dilute the drink. Strain into a small Champagne coupe and add the garnish.

Yellow Parrot

1 oz / 3 cl	yellow Chartreuse
⅔ oz / 2 cl	apricot brandy
⅔ oz / 2 cl	anisette

Combine the ingredients in a shaker with ice and shake. Strain into a chilled cocktail glass.

basil

Known to be good for the brain, basil imparts a delicious aroma to a cocktail. The usual basil flavor is herbaceous and sweet with a slight hint of licorice.

Basil Martini

2 oz / 6 cl	basil vodka
½ oz / 1.5 cl	dry vermouth
dash	simple syrup (page 20)
3	fresh basil leaves
GARNISH	basil leaf

Combine the ingredients in a shaker with ice and shake hard to bruise the basil leaves. Strain into a chilled cocktail glass. Add the garnish.

Euphoria Cocktail

1⅔ oz / 5 cl	basil vodka
½ oz / 1.5 cl	wild strawberry liqueur
½ oz / 1.5 cl	Parfait Amour
dash	fresh lemon juice
2	fresh purple basil leaves
GARNISH	purple basil leaf sprayed very lightly with CK Euphoria for Men

Combine the ingredients in a shaker with ice and shake hard to bruise the basil leaves. Double-strain into a chilled cocktail glass. Float the garnish on top of the drink. This gives an incredible aroma to the drink.

Oriental Tea Party

2 oz / 6 cl	vodka
1 oz / 3 cl	apple juice
½ oz / 1.5 cl	fresh lime juice
½ oz / 1.5 cl	cranberry juice
4	basil leaves
GARNISH	thin wedge of apple, basil leaf

Combine the ingredients in a shaker with ice and shake hard to bruise the basil leaves. Strain into an old-fashioned glass filled with ice. Add the garnish.

bénédictine

An old herbal remedy that became a popular after-dinner drink, Bénédictine is made from twenty-seven plants and spices. It has a honey flavor with hints of medicinal bitter herb and orange.

B & B

1 oz / 3 cl	brandy
1 oz / 3 cl	Bénédictine

Pour the ingredients into a brandy snifter and stir.

Bobby Burns

2 oz / 6 cl	Scotch whisky
1 oz / 3 cl	Bénédictine
½ oz / 1.5 cl	red vermouth

GARNISH   twist of orange

Combine the ingredients in a mixing glass with ice and stir. Strain into a chilled cocktail glass. Add the garnish.

Brainstorm

1⅔ oz / 5 cl	bourbon
1 oz / 3 cl	Bénédictine
½ oz / 1.5 cl	dry vermouth

GARNISH   twist of lemon

Combine the ingredients in a mixing glass with ice and stir. Strain into a chilled cocktail glass. Add the garnish.

cilantro

An herb of the parsley family, cilantro has a pungent citrus flavor with a faint undertone of anise and a biting tang. Be sure you don't inadvertently pick up flat-leaf parsley, which looks similar.

Deep Thinker

1²⁄₃ oz / 5 cl	spiced rum
½ oz / 1.5 cl	elderflower cordial
1	lime, diced
6	cilantro sprigs
1½ tsps	demarara sugar

Muddle the lime, cilantro, and sugar in the bottom of an old-fashioned glass. Add crushed ice and the remaining ingredients and stir.

Limeade

1½ oz / 4.5 cl	Licor 43
½ oz / 1.5 cl	elderflower cordial
½ oz / 1.5 cl	vanilla syrup (page 24)
handful	fresh cilantro

Muddle the cilantro with the vanilla syrup in the bottom of an old-fashioned glass. Add the elderflower cordial. Fill the glass with crushed ice. Add the Licor 43 and stir. Add more crushed ice.

Mellow Yellow

2 oz / 6 cl	gin
²⁄₃ oz / 2 cl	limoncello
⅓ oz / 1 cl	fresh lemon juice
4 or 5	fresh cilantro leaves
	lemon sorbet
GARNISH	sprig of cilantro

Combine the ingredients in a shaker with ice and shake hard to bruise the cilantro leaves. Strain into a Champagne coupe over a scoop of lemon sorbet. Add the garnish.

elderflower

The cordial made from this flower has a delicate, scented flavor. In liqueur form, it has Riesling and Muscat grape aromas; after that, some gooseberry and green plum notes emerge with intense and beguiling flavors of tangerine, tropical fruit, and persimmon.

Elderflower Collins

1²⁄₃ oz / 5 cl	gin
¾ oz / 2.5 cl	elderflower cordial
¾ oz / 2.5 cl	fresh lemon juice
1 tsp	simple syrup (page 20)
	club soda
GARNISH	wedge of lemon

Combine all the ingredients except the club soda in a shaker with ice and shake. Strain into a highball filled with crushed ice. Top up with soda and stir. Add the garnish.

Elderflower Margarita

1²⁄₃ oz / 5 cl	silver tequila
²⁄₃ oz / 2 cl	elderflower cordial
²⁄₃ oz / 2 cl	apple juice
½ oz / 1.5 cl	fresh lime juice
GARNISH	wedge of lime

Combine the ingredients in a shaker with ice and shake. Strain into a chilled cocktail glass. Slit the lime and place it on the rim of the glass.

Sal's St. Germain

1²⁄₃ oz / 5 cl	St. Germain elderflower liqueur
½ oz / 1.5 cl	fresh lemon juice
½ oz / 1.5 cl	orange juice
dash	Peychaud's orange bitters
dash	pasteurized egg white
GARNISH	elderflower blossom or twist of orange

Combine the ingredients in a shaker with ice and shake. Strain into an old-fashioned glass filled with ice. Add the garnish.

hibiscus

The wild hibiscus flower has a tart taste with a raspberry, rhubarb, and plum character. Because of its vibrant red color, it livens up a cocktail. Hibiscus flowers in syrup are available commercially (see Sources, page 191), or the syrup can be made at home using dried hibiscus flowers.

Hibiscus Daiquiri

2 oz / 6 cl	light rum
1 oz / 3 cl	fresh lime juice
1 oz / 3 cl	wild hibiscus syrup
1	hibiscus flower from the jar
GARNISH	slice of lime

Place the flower upright in a chilled cocktail glass. Combine the remaining ingredients in a shaker with ice and shake. Strain into the prepared glass and add the garnish.

Hibiscus Kiss

1 oz / 3 cl	pear vodka
½ oz / 1.5 cl	elderflower liqueur
½ oz / 1.5 cl	hibiscus syrup
	Champagne
GARNISH	hibiscus flower

Combine all the ingredients except the Champagne in a shaker with ice and shake. Strain into a Champagne flute, top up with Champagne, and stir. Add the garnish.

Hibiscus Margarita

2 oz / 6 cl	reposado tequila
1 oz / 3 cl	fresh lime juice
½ oz / 1.5 cl	hibiscus syrup
GARNISH	hibiscus flower

Combine the ingredients in a shaker with ice and shake. Strain into a chilled Champagne coupe. Add the garnish.

Hibiscus Sour

2 oz / 6 cl	rye whiskey
1 oz / 3 cl	fresh lemon juice
½ oz / 1.5 cl	hibiscus syrup
1	egg white
GARNISH	hibiscus flower

Combine the ingredients in a shaker with ice and shake. Strain into a chilled Champagne coupe. Add the garnish.

lavender

The taste of lavender is delicate and subtly spicy;
it adds piquancy to a cocktail. Be sure the lavender
buds you use are organic, or at least unsprayed.

À Vous de Savourer

1 oz / 3 cl	Genever gin
1 oz / 3 cl	fresh grapefruit juice
½ oz / 1.5 cl	lavender syrup (page 22)
dash	orange bitters
	Champagne
GARNISH	lavender sprig

Combine all the ingredients except the
Champagne in a shaker with ice and shake.
Strain into a Champagne coupe. Top up with
Champagne and stir. Add the garnish.

Lavenderita

1⅓ oz / 4 cl	tequila
½ oz / 1.5 cl	Parfait Amour
1 tsp	peach liqueur
2 tsps	simple syrup (page 20)
1	fresh lavender flower
GARNISH	stem of lavender

Muddle the lavender flower in the bottom of
a shaker. Add ice and the remaining ingredients and shake. Double-strain into a chilled
cocktail glass. Add the garnish.

Lavender Mojito

2 oz / 6 cl	Charbay rum or vanilla rum
1 oz / 3 cl	fresh lime juice
1 oz / 3 cl	simple syrup (page 20)
3	fresh lavender flowers
5	mint leaves
	club soda
GARNISH	stem of lavender

Muddle the mint and lavender with the lime
juice and simple syrup in the bottom of a
mixing glass. Add ice and the rum and stir.
Pour into a highball filled with ice. Top up
with club soda and stir. Add the garnish.

lemongrass

An Asian ingredient, the pale-looking lemongrass has
segued into the cocktail bar. It has a light lemon flavor,
as its name suggests. Buy it as fresh as you can.

Grace

1²⁄₃ oz / 5 cl	pear vodka
1²⁄₃ oz / 5 cl	fresh pear juice
1²⁄₃ oz / 5 cl	fresh apple juice
¾ oz / 2.5 cl	fresh lemon juice
1 tsp	honey syrup (page 22)
1½ inch / 4 cm	piece lemongrass
4 or 5	mint leaves
GARNISH	lemongrass straw*, sprig of mint

Cut the lemongrass into 4 or 5 pieces and
muddle them in the bottom of a shaker. Add
ice and the remaining ingredients and shake.
Strain into a highball filled with crushed ice. A
few particles of mint and lemongrass will pass
through the filter. Add the garnish.

*To make a lemongrass straw, trim a piece of
lemongrass about 1 inch shorter than a plastic
straw. Insert the straw into the lemongrass,.
(Peel the skin back from the lemongrass. It
will then easily wrap around the straw.)

Cool, refreshing elegance,
Grace has great texture
for a long drink. ❯ ❯ ❯

Lemongrass Collins

1²⁄₃ oz / 5 cl	lemongrass-infused vodka
2 in / 5 cm	piece lemongrass
¾ oz / 2.5 cl	fresh lemon juice
½ oz / 1.5 cl	simple syrup (page 20)
	club soda
GARNISH	lemongrass tubes, mint leaves, orange twist

Muddle lemongrass in the bottom of a shaker.
Add vodka, lemon juice, and simple syrup
and shake. Double-strain into a highball filled
with ice. Top up with club soda and stir. Add
the garnish.

mint

There are a few different types of mint, but the most common
is the refreshing spearmint. When buying fresh mint, look
for perky, bright green leaves with no signs of wilting.

Bourbon Pick-Me-Up

1½ oz / 4.5 cl	bourbon
½ oz / 1.5 cl	Branca Menthe
½ oz / 1.5 cl	fresh lemon juice
8	mint leaves
GARNISH	mint sprig

Combine the ingredients in a shaker with ice
and shake hard to bruise the mint. Double-
strain into an old-fashioned glass filled with
ice. Add the garnish.

Mojito

1¾ oz / 5 cl	light rum
⅔ oz / 2 cl	fresh lime juice
1	sprig fresh mint
1 tsp	superfine (caster) sugar
	sparkling water

Gently muddle the mint with the sugar and
lime juice in the bottom of a highball. Add
the rum, fill with crushed ice, top up with
sparkling water, and stir. Serve with a straw.

Mint Julep

1⅔ oz / 5 cl	bourbon
1 tsp	superfine (caster) sugar
1 tsp	cold water
bunch	fresh mint leaves
GARNISH	sprig of mint

Muddle the mint with the sugar and water
in the bottom of an old-fashioned glass until
the sugar is dissolved. Add the bourbon. Fill
the glass with crushed ice and stir. Add the
garnish. Serve with a straw and stirrer.

oregano

With its strong and gutsy herbal flavor, oregano goes well with lemon. It has a peppery bite to it, which comes through even when the herb is combined with many other flavors.

Gin and Sin

6 oz / 2 cl	Hendrick's gin
1.5 cl / ½ oz	Noilly Prat
2	thick slices of cucumber (½ inch / 1 cm)
½	teaspoon dried oregano
GARNISH	slice of cucumber

Muddle the cucumber in the bottom of a shaker. Add the remaining ingredients and ice and shake. Double-strain into an old-fashioned glass filled with ice. Add the garnish.

Scubarello

1⅔ oz / 5 cl	vodka
⅓ oz / 1 cl	crème de framboise
⅓ oz / 1 cl	crème de mûre
⅔ oz / 2 cl	fresh lime juice
1	fresh stem oregano
3	raspberries
3	blackberries
1 tsp	demerara sugar
	club soda
GARNISH	raspberry, blackberry, tip of oregano

Muddle the berries with the sugar and oregano in the bottom of a shaker. Add ice and the remaining ingredients except the soda. Shake well. Strain into a highball filled with ice. Top up with soda. Add the garnish.

rose

The petals of a rose are softly fragrant, with a flavor to match.
Pure rose essence is more intense than rose water, offering
a beautiful floral bouquet. Both are available commercially.
Still, a spirit infused with rose petals tastes different.

Desert Rose

2 oz / 6 cl	gin infused with rose*
¾ oz / 2.5 cl	fresh lemon juice
½ oz / 1.5 cl	pear puree
½ oz / 1.5 cl	simple syrup (page 20)

GARNISH pink rose petal

Combine the ingredients in a shaker with ice
and shake. Strain into a chilled coupe glass
and add the garnish.

*Add 1 oz / 3 cl dried rose bud tea to 1 bottle
gin and set aside at room temperature for at
least 2 hours to infuse. Strain through muslin,
then bottle.

La Rosita

2 oz / 6 cl	light rum
½ oz / 1.5 cl	peach puree
½ oz / 1.5 cl	rose water
1 tsp	simple syrup (page 20)
1	small piece fresh cucumber

GARNISH white rose petal

Muddle the cucumber in the bottom of a
shaker. Add ice and the remaining ingredients
and shake. Double-strain into a chilled cocktail glass. Add the garnish.

Heebie

1⅔ oz / 5 cl	rose vodka
⅔ oz / 2 cl	triple sec
1 oz / 3 cl	pomegranate juice
dash	rose water

GARNISH pink rose petals

Combine the ingredients in a shaker with ice
and shake. Strain into a chilled cocktail glass.
Add the garnish.

rosemary

A familiar herb, rosemary presents the nose with
a woodsy aroma and a hint of pine. It is mintlike,
yet sweeter, with a slight ginger finish. It is good
in a cocktail when used as a subtle accent.

Rosa Maria

2 oz / 6 cl	silver tequila
½ oz / 1.5 cl	Cointreau
1 oz / 3 cl	fresh lime juice
1 oz / 3 cl	agave syrup
1	sprig fresh rosemary
GARNISH	sprig of rosemary

Muddle the rosemary with the syrup in the
bottom of a shaker. Add ice and the remaining
ingredients and shake. Double-strain into a
chilled cocktail glass. Add the garnish.

Rosemary Cooler

2 oz / 6 cl	vodka
½ oz / 1.5 cl	mango syrup (page 22)
½ oz / 1.5 cl	fresh lime juice
1⅓ oz / 4 cl	blood orange juice
dash	grenadine
1	sprig fresh rosemary
GARNISH	sprig of rosemary, wedge of orange

Muddle the rosemary in the bottom of a
shaker. Add ice and the remaining ingredients
and shake. Double-strain into a highball filled
with crushed ice. Add the garnish.

Rosemary-tini

2 oz / 6 cl	rosemary-infused vodka*
½ oz / 1.5 cl	dry vermouth
dash	Pernod
GARNISH	sprig of rosemary

Combine the ingredients in a shaker with ice
and shake. Strain into a chilled cocktail glass.
Add the garnish.

*Infuse the vodka with a generous bunch of
fresh rosemary for at least 48 hours, until the
flavor is established in the spirit, and strain
into a clean bottle.

sage

Its soft green-gray leaves are big and flat, making them easy to chop.
When touched, the plant releases a woody, earthy scent into the air.

La Salvación Cocktail

1½ oz / 4.5 cl	white rum
½ oz / 1.5 cl	yellow Chartreuse
½ oz / 1.5 cl	Falernum liqueur
1 oz / 3 cl	fresh lime juice
3	sage leaves
GARNISH	sage leaf

Combine the ingredients in a shaker with
ice and shake. Double-strain into a chilled
Champagne coupe and add the garnish.

Sage Fan

1⅔ oz / 5 cl	vodka
⅔ oz / 2 cl	limoncello
1 oz / 3 cl	apple juice
dash	honey syrup (page 22)
dash	fresh lemon juice
3	fresh sage leaves, torn
GARNISH	apple fan (see page 15), sage leaves

Combine the ingredients in a shaker with ice
and shake. Strain into an old-fashioned glass
filled with ice. Add the apple fan with sage
leaves inserted in the middle of it. Serve with
a straw.

‹ ‹ ‹ The star of **Rosemary Cooler** is the
long sprig of rosemary, which adds even
more flavor.

Sage Love

1⅔ oz / 5 cl	light rum
⅔ oz / 2 cl	Mandarine Napoleon liqueur
½ oz / 1.5 cl	fresh lime juice
1⅔ oz / 5 cl	pineapple juice
1⅔ oz / 5 cl	passion fruit juice
4	fresh sage leaves, torn
GARNISH	sage leaves

Combine the ingredients in a shaker with
ice and shake. Double-strain into an old-
fashioned glass filled with ice. Add the
garnish. Serve with a straw.

tea

Traditional green and black teas, made from the leaves of the tea plant, offer a wide variety of aromatics and lend themselves very well to the art of cocktail making. There are also endless flavor possibilities in herbal teas, which are infusions of dried herbs and flowers.

Fingertips

1⅔ oz / 5 cl	rosé vermouth*
¾ oz / 2.5 cl	Cointreau
½ oz / 1.5 cl	fresh lime juice
½ oz / 1.5 cl	cranberry juice
GARNISH	rose petal

Combine the ingredients in a shaker with ice and shake. Strain into a chilled cocktail glass and add the garnish.

*To infuse the rosé vermouth: Carefully wash and dry ¾ cup white rose petals. Combine petals and a bottle of rosé vermouth in a bowl and let infuse for 2 days. Fine-strain and bottle to use as needed.

Hanoi

1½ oz / 4.5 cl	golden rum
½ oz / 1.5 cl	Campari
½ oz / 1.5 cl	fresh lime juice
1 oz / 3 cl	cold green tea
1½ tsps	clear honey
GARNISH	wedge of lime

Combine the ingredients in a shaker with ice and shake. Strain into an old-fashioned glass filled with ice. Add the garnish.

Kentucky Derby Cooler

1⅔ oz / 5 cl	bourbon
3 oz / 9 cl	strong breakfast tea
⅔ oz / 2 cl	maple syrup
1	lemon wedge
1	large orange wedge
1	small mint sprig
GARNISH	sprig of mint

Squeeze the juice from the fruit into a shaker and discard the wedges. Add ice and the remaining ingredients and shake. Strain into a highball filled with ice. Add the garnish.

Kentucky Iced Tea

1½ oz / 4.5 cl	bourbon
½ oz / 1.5 cl	vanilla liqueur
⅔ oz / 2 cl	fresh lemon juice
2 oz / 6 cl	cold unsweetened iced tea
6	fresh mint leaves
1 tsp	superfine (caster) sugar
GARNISH	sprig of mint

Combine all the ingredients except the tea in a shaker with ice and shake. Double-strain into a highball filled with ice, top up with the tea, and stir. Add the garnish.

Spank the Monkey

1²⁄₃ oz / 5 cl	white vermouth
⅓ oz / 1 cl	Bénédictine ginseng spirit
²⁄₃ oz / 2 cl	pink grapefruit juice
⅓ oz / 1 cl	vanilla syrup (page 24)
1⅓ oz / 4 cl	black currant tea
	Champagne

Combine all the ingredients except the Champagne in a shaker with ice and shake. Strain into a chilled wine glass filled with ice and top up with the Champagne.

Teatime Cocktail

1 oz / 3 cl	Hendrick's gin
8 oz / 24 cl	hot green tea
dash	fresh lemon juice
1 tsp	superfine (caster) sugar
1	lime zest
1	cinnamon stick

Combine the gin, lemon juice, and lime peel in a teacup or heatproof glass. Add the hot tea and sugar. Stir with the cinnamon stick and serve.

The Southern Promise

1²⁄₃ oz / 5 cl	dark rum infused with Moroccan mint tea*
⅓ oz / 1 cl	rhum agricole
⅓ oz / 1 cl	mezcal
½ oz / 1.5 cl	fresh lemon juice
1½ tsps	lavender syrup (page 22)
3 drops	Angostura bitters
GARNISH	sprig of lavender

Combine the ingredients in a shaker with ice and shake. Strain into a Champagne coupe and add the garnish.

*To infuse the dark rum: Put 2 tsps of Moroccan mint tea, 1 tsp of dried peppermint, and 5 oz / 15 cl of dark rum into a catering creaming siphon. Charge with two N_2O cartridges and let infuse for 10 minutes. Release pressure and fine-strain.

thyme

The flavor has been described as delicately herbal with a faint clove aftertaste. Lemon thyme has a lemony zest to it and, like all other thyme flavors, is extra pungent when fresh.

Evening Thyme

1½ oz / 4.5 cl	vodka
⅔ oz / 2 cl	Lillet Rouge
⅓ oz / 1 cl	triple sec
2 dashes	Angostura bitters
1	fresh thyme sprig
GARNISH	sprig of thyme

Combine the ingredients in a shaker with ice and shake hard to bruise the thyme. Double-strain into a chilled cocktail glass. Add the garnish.

Spring Thyme

1½ oz / 4.5 cl	vodka
1 oz / 3 cl	limoncello
1 oz / 3 cl	green apple puree
1 oz / 3 cl	thyme syrup (page 22)
1 oz / 3 cl	fresh lime juice
GARNISH	sprig of thyme

Combine the ingredients in a shaker with ice and shake. Strain into an old-fashioned glass filled with ice. Add the garnish across the top of the drink.

Perfect Thyme

2½ oz / 6.5 cl	gin
2 or 3	small slices fresh ginger
2 or 3	slices lemongrass stalk
1	fresh thyme sprig

Muddle the ginger, lemongrass, and thyme in a mixing glass. Add ice cubes, then the gin. Stir to combine all flavors. Strain into a chilled cocktail glass.

violet

This intensely perfumed little flower is widely used in culinary arts, both sweet and savory. The French use viola essence to flavor their violet liqueurs, which are very sweet and have an intense purple color. They are best used with white spirits to maintain their delicious aroma and color.

Aviation

1²/₃ oz / 5 cl	gin
²/₃ oz / 1 cl	crème de violette
²/₃ oz / 1 cl	maraschino liqueur
½ oz / 1.5 cl	fresh lemon juice

Combine the ingredients in a shaker with ice and shake. Strain into a chilled cocktail glass.

Diamond Royal Jubilee

1½ oz / 4.5 cl	gin infused with white rose, frozen*
²/₃ oz / 2 cl	crème de violette
²/₃ oz / 2 cl	Champagne
4	white roses
GARNISH	white rose petal

Combine the gin and crème de violette in a mixing glass with ice and stir. Strain into a chilled Champagne coupe, pour the Champagne on top, and gently stir. Add the garnish.

*Rinse and dry the white rose petals and add to a bottle of gin. Rest the bottle on its side and leave for one week at room temperature. Pour the gin through a sieve into a clean bottle and place in the freezer for 24 hours.

Lady Violette

1½ oz / 4.5 cl	gin
½ oz / 1.5 cl	Cointreau
½ oz / 1.5 cl	crème de violette
½ oz / 1.5 cl	fresh lemon juice
1	egg white
GARNISH	violet flower

Combine the ingredients in a shaker with ice and shake. Strain into a chilled Champagne coupe and add the garnish.

nut flavors

The world of flavor would be less interesting if there were no subtle nut flavors. Take the almond, for example. There are two kinds of almonds: the bitter almond from Asia and the Mediterranean region, and the sweet almond, of which more than a hundred varieties are grown in California alone.

Drinkers of amaretto, considered by some to be the king of nut-flavored liqueurs, will already know its bitter almond flavor, but most people don't know that amaretto is made primarily from apricot kernels—the soft seed inside an apricot pit. Likewise, you can taste almond in crème de noyaux, a liqueur made from almonds or peach or apricot kernels. Pink in color, it is a fine alternative to amaretto in some drinks. Almonds themselves may be flaked or slivered as a garnish.

From the Piedmont region of Italy, Frangelico liqueur is made with toasted wild hazelnuts, combined with cocoa and vanilla, rhubarb root, and sweet orange flowers, plus other natural flavors. Add to this a period in fine oak casks to mature, and you have a golden, smooth liqueur that is especially tasty. You can serve it straight, chilled, over ice, in a cocktail, or mixed with tonic or club soda.

Walnuts are used in crème de noix, a liqueur prized for its slightly sweet flavor. It also includes honey and is sometimes called eau-de-vie de noix.

The everlasting appeal of a nut-flavored liqueur lies in the mellow, sweet flavor, full body, and interesting, lingering aftertaste.

Nut liqueurs are great mixers in after-dinner cocktails, and if that's your taste, then you'll be nuts about these recipes.

almond

When combined with other ingredients, the nutty almond flavor comes through on the finish. Light and slightly sweet, this is an intriguing but subtle flavor.

Mai Tai

2 oz / 6 cl	aged rum
²⁄₃ oz / 2 cl	orange curaçao
²⁄₃ oz / 2 cl	fresh lime juice
²⁄₃ oz / 2 cl	orgeat
GARNISH	wedge of lime, sprig of mint

Combine the ingredients in a shaker with ice and shake. Strain into an old-fashioned glass filled with ice. Add the garnish on a cocktail stick.

Tara Special

²⁄₃ oz / 2 cl	amaretto
²⁄₃ oz / 2 cl	white peach puree
1 dash	fresh orange juice
3	raspberries
	Prosecco
GARNISH	raspberries, mint leaf

Combine all the ingredients except the Prosecco in a shaker with ice and shake. Strain into a chilled Champagne flute. Top up with Prosecco. Add the garnish on a cocktail stick.

Tennessee Squirrel has a delicate passion fruit flavor. ❯ ❯ ❯

Tennessee Squirrel

1²⁄₃ oz / 5 cl	Jack Daniels
¾ oz / 2.5 cl	amaretto
²⁄₃ oz / 2 cl	fresh lemon juice
2 dashes	passion fruit syrup (page 22)
1	passion fruit
GARNISH	quarter of a passion fruit

Scoop the flesh of the passion fruit into a shaker. Add the remaining ingredients and ice and shake. Strain into an old-fashioned glass filled with ice, allowing some of the fruit to pass through to add texture to the drink. Add the garnish on a cocktail stick across the top of the glass.

coffee

Freshly ground coffee flavors can vary greatly. Sweet, salty, bitter, and sour tastes are perceived on the tongue. Coffee liqueurs such as Kahlúa have a thick consistency and mix well.

Black Russian

| 1⅓ oz / 4 cl | vodka |
| ⅔ oz / 2 cl | Kahlúa |

Pour the vodka into an old-fashioned glass filled with ice. Add the Kahlúa and stir. Serve with a stirrer.

Espresso Martini

2 oz / 6 cl	vodka
½ oz / 1.5 cl	Kahlúa
1 oz / 3 cl	espresso coffee
GARNISH	4 coffee beans

Combine the ingredients in a shaker with ice and shake. Strain into a chilled cocktail glass. Float the garnish on top of the drink.

Irish Coffee

1⅔ oz / 5 cl	Irish whiskey
2 tsps	brown sugar
3 oz / 9 cl	hot coffee
⅔ oz / 2 cl	heavy cream

Pour the whiskey into a heatproof glass. Add the sugar and stir. Add the hot coffee and stir. Gently pour the cream over the back of a bar spoon so it creates a separate layer on top of the drink.

Last Sin

1⅔ oz / 5 cl	aged rum
1 oz / 3 cl	Frangelico
⅓ oz / 1 cl	simple syrup (page 20)
1 shot	espresso coffee
GARNISH	3 coffee beans

Combine the ingredients in a shaker with ice and shake. Strain into a chilled cocktail glass. Float the garnish on top of the drink.

Black Russian (foreground) and **Last Sin** cocktails are full of coffee flavor. 〉 〉 〉

hazelnut

The flavor of toasted hazelnuts fills the mouth when you taste hazelnut liqueur in a cocktail. It also delivers a full-bodied texture to further enhance the combination.

Fosbury Flip

1½ oz / 4.5 cl	aged rum
½ oz / 1.5 cl	Frangelico
½ oz / 1.5 cl	apricot brandy
2 oz / 6 cl	fresh orange juice
½ oz / 1.5 cl	fresh lime juice
dash	grenadine
1	fresh egg yolk (pasteurized)

GARNISH   grated orange zest

Combine the ingredients in a shaker with ice and shake. Strain into a highball filled with ice. Add the garnish.

Hazelnut-ini

2 oz / 6 cl	vodka
⅔ oz / 2 cl	Frangelico
dash	crème de cacao

GARNISH   orange spiral

Combine the ingredients in a shaker with ice and shake. Strain into a chilled cocktail glass. Add the garnish.

Frenzy

1 oz / 3 cl	hazelnut liqueur
½ oz / 1.5 cl	Aperol
1 oz / 3 cl	limoncello
½ oz / 1.5 cl	fresh lemon juice
dash	grenadine
1	fresh egg yolk (pasteurized)

Combine the ingredients in a shaker with ice and shake. Strain into an old-fashioned glass filled with ice.

Hazelnut flavor dominates in this **Hazelnut-tini** that is enhanced by an orange spiral garnish. 〉〉〉

spices

The small, red hot chile is one of my favorite spices. It not only looks exotic on the rim of a glass (such as in the Spicy Fifty cocktail on page 149), but it also delivers the hot and spicy sensation needed to wake up the mouth. However, not all chiles are piercingly hot. I like the jalapeño, which is a moderately hot chile, for dicing and muddling, and the bird's eye, which is hotter, for decoration. There are hundreds of types of chile, some hot, some milder—if you use the variety listed in the recipes, you will not give your palate too much of a hot surprise.

You can use spices in cocktails as an infusion or as a fresh spice muddled or shaken with other ingredients. The key to using a spicy flavor is to hint at it and not overwhelm all else in the mix, so look for balance.

Of the other spices in this section, ginger is one that's perhaps already familiar to drinkers of hot and spicy cocktails, the kind you sip when it's cold. However, fresh ginger has a zingy flavor, and pieces of it are often muddled or used for infusion in contemporary and healthy cocktails available in bars today.

Cinnamon sticks are also great in hot drinks and for infusions. You can also sprinkle grated cinnamon or nutmeg over the top of a creamy cocktail to give it a spice aroma.

The idea of saffron as a cocktail ingredient is unusual, but it is a great flavor for mixing with an herb such as tarragon and an orange curaçao liqueur.

The vanilla recipes here make use of three different forms of vanilla: vanilla liqueur, vanilla vodka, and vanilla syrup. Each is combined with a variety of fruits and spirits to let the vanilla flavor shine through.

chile

The flavor of chiles ranges from mild to very hot, depending on the type you select. For cocktails, use the smaller bird's eye chile, if you can find it, or the usual red chile. The flavor is concentrated at the top of the pepper. Chiles are rich in vitamin C and high in potassium, magnesium, and iron.

Hot Gringo

2 oz / 6 cl	añejo (aged) tequila
1 oz / 3 cl	fresh lime juice
½ oz / 1.5 cl	lemongrass syrup (page 22)
3	thin slices chile
GARNISH	wedge of lime

Combine the ingredients in a shaker with ice and shake. Strain into a chilled cocktail glass. Add the garnish.

Love, Honor & Obey

1⅔ oz / 5 cl	vanilla vodka
⅓ oz / 1 cl	fresh lime juice
1 tsp	honey
1	lemongrass stalk, diced
¾ cup	diced watermelon
2	thin slices bird's eye chile

Muddle the lemongrass, watermelon, chile, and honey in the bottom of a shaker. Add ice and the vodka and lime juice and shake. Double-strain into a chilled cocktail glass.

Spicy Fifty

1⅔ oz / 5 cl	vanilla vodka
½ oz / 1.5 cl	elderflower cordial
⅔ oz / 2 cl	fresh lime juice
⅓ oz / 1 cl	honey syrup (page 22)
2	thin slices of red chile
GARNISH	bird's eye chile

Combine the ingredients in a shaker with ice and shake. Strain into a chilled cocktail glass. Slit the chile and place it on the rim of the glass.

Stealth Margarita

2 oz / 6 cl	tequila
1 oz / 3 cl	Grand Marnier
½ oz / 1.5 cl	elderflower cordial
2 cubes	frozen lemon juice
GARNISH	small green chile

Combine all the ingredients except the lemon juice in a mixing glass with ice and stir. Place the lemon ice cubes in a chilled cocktail glass and strain the mixture over the cubes. Split the chile to expose the seeds and slide it around the rim of the glass to add a hint of heat.

cinnamon

This is the dried inner bark of a tree in the laurel family, and it has a sweet, woody flavor that is familiar to us in hot teas and buns. It is available in stick form and ground.

Big Kiss

1²⁄₃ oz / 5 cl	vanilla vodka
½ oz / 1.5 cl	crème de noisette
1 oz / 3 cl	Goldschläger cinnamon schnapps
½ oz / 1.5 cl	chilled mineral water
GARNISH	cinnamon stick

Combine the ingredients in a shaker with ice and shake. Strain into a chilled cocktail glass. Add the garnish across the top of the glass.

Golden Jubilee

1⅓ oz / 4 cl	gin
½ oz / 1.5 cl	Goldschläger cinnamon schnapps
½ oz / 1.5 cl	Parfait Amour
	Champagne

Combine all the ingredients except the Champagne in a mixing glass with ice and stir. Strain into a chilled cocktail glass. Top up with Champagne.

Cinnamon May

1½ oz / 4.5 cl	vodka
½ oz / 1.5 cl	kiwi liqueur
½ oz / 1.5 cl	cinnamon syrup (page 20)
2	kumquats, diced
GARNISH	cinnamon stick

Muddle the kumquats in the bottom of a shaker. Add ice and the remaining ingredients and shake. Double-strain into a chilled cocktail glass. Add the garnish.

ginger

I like to use fresh ginger in cocktails because of its sharp, clean flavor. It adds a zing to any drink when used in the right proportion. Young ginger is juicy and fleshy with a mild taste. Its essential oils contain the fragrance.

Ginger Nut

1⅓ oz / 4 cl	gin
½ oz / 1.5 cl	crème de noisette
½ oz / 1.5 cl	caramel liqueur
1⅓ oz / 4 cl	fresh orange juice
1 tsp	minced fresh ginger (or powdered)
	ginger beer
GARNISH	two thin slices of ginger, tip of mint

Combine all the ingredients except the ginger beer in a shaker with ice and shake. Strain into a highball filled with ice. Top up with ginger beer and stir. Add the garnish.

Moscow Mule

1⅔ oz / 5 cl	vodka
⅔ oz / 2 cl	fresh lime juice
	ginger beer
GARNISH	wedge of lime

Combine the vodka and lime juice in a highball filled with ice. Top up with ginger beer and stir. Add the garnish.

Rama

1½ oz / 4.5 cl	tequila
½ oz / 1.5 cl	Mandarine Napoleon liqueur
½ oz / 1.5 cl	cranberry juice
½ oz / 1.5 cl	ginger syrup (page 21)
	fine sea salt
	wedge of lime
GARNISH	wedge of lime

Use the salt and the wedge of lime to crust half the rim of a chilled cocktail glass (see page 14). Combine the ingredients in a shaker with ice and shake. Strain into the glass. Slit the lime wedge and place it on the rim of the glass.

pepper

This is the king of spices and is excellent for your digestion. Peppercorns may be black, green, pink, or white, but black peppercorns have the strongest flavor. They have a warm aroma and a spicy flavor.

Arabian Dream

1⅓ oz / 4 cl	honey vodka
½ oz / 1.5 cl	lime juice
2 oz / 6 cl	fresh apple juice
dash	grenadine
5 twists	black pepper
GARNISH	lime spiral, ground pepper

Combine the ingredients in a shaker with ice and shake. Strain into a highball filled with crushed ice. Add the garnish.

Grand Pepper

1¾ oz / 5 cl	vodka
⅔ oz / 2 cl	Grand Marnier
⅓ oz / 1 cl	strawberry liqueur
GARNISH	½ tsp crushed pink peppercorns

Combine the ingredients in a shaker with ice and shake. Strain into a chilled cocktail glass. Crush a few pink peppercorns and sprinkle the garnish over the top.

Snap, Crackle, Drop

1½ oz / 4.5 cl	reposado tequila
7 or 8 dashes	Angostura bitters
4 or 5 twists	freshly ground black pepper
	wedge of lime

On a saucer, combine the bitters and pepper and mix until it turns into a paste. Coat one side of the lime wedge with the paste. Pour the tequila into a shot glass and place the lime wedge on top. Bite on the lime and then sip the tequila for a unique taste experience.

❮ ❮ ❮ An **Arabian Dream** has spicy pepper on the nose and a lime spiral for visual effect.

saffron

Bright yellow in color, saffron has a strong perfume and a bitter, honeylike taste. It is pleasantly spicy and can linger on the palate.

Mayfair Fizz No. 2

1 oz / 3 cl	Bénédictine
1 oz / 3 cl	white grapefruit juice
	white of 1 quail egg
1 tsp	agave syrup
pinch	soft sea salt (such as Maldon)
pinch	saffron threads
	Champagne
GARNISH	twist of grapefruit, pinch of saffron

Combine all the ingredients except the Champagne in a shaker filled with ice and shake. Strain into a highball filled with ice. Top up with Champagne and stir. Add the garnish.

Saffron Love

1⅔ oz / 5 cl	vodka
½ oz / 1.5 cl	orange curaçao liqueur
½ oz / 1.5 cl	saffron syrup (page 23)
½ oz / 1.5 cl	fresh orange juice
½ oz / 1.5 cl	honey syrup (page 22)
GARNISH	twist of orange

Combine the ingredients in a shaker with ice and shake. Strain into a chilled cocktail glass. Add the garnish.

Saffron Sour

2 oz / 6 cl	saffron gin
1 oz / 3 cl	fresh lemon juice
½ oz / 1.5 cl	simple syrup (page 20)
1	egg white
dash	orange bitters
GARNISH	pinch of saffron

Combine the ingredients in a shaker with ice and shake. Strain into a chilled cocktail glass and add the garnish.

vanilla

Vanilla is one of the most complex flavors, with hundreds of components that create its taste and aroma. Smooth and creamy describes most vanillas.

Barbie

1²⁄₃ oz / 5 cl	gin
½ oz / 1.5 cl	rhubarb puree
1 oz / 3 cl	vanilla syrup (page 24)
dash	gooseberry syrup (page 21)
GARNISH	gooseberry

Combine the ingredients in a shaker with ice and shake. Strain into a chilled cocktail glass. Add the garnish on a cocktail stick.

Cocktail Bon-bon

1²⁄₃ oz / 5 cl	vanilla vodka
½ oz / 1.5 cl	butterscotch schnapps
½ oz / 1.5 cl	limoncello
½ oz / 1.5 cl	fresh lemon juice
1 tsp	vanilla sugar
GARNISH	Morello cherry

Combine the ingredients in a shaker with ice and shake. Strain into an old-fashioned glass filled with ice and add the garnish.

Porn Star Martini

1½ oz / 4.5 cl	vanilla vodka
½ oz / 1.5 cl	Passoa liqueur
	flesh of 1 fresh passion fruit
2 tsps	vanilla sugar
	Champagne
GARNISH	slice of passion fruit

Combine all the ingredients except the Champagne in a shaker with ice and shake. Double-strain into a chilled cocktail glass and add the garnish. Serve with Champagne on the side in a chilled shot glass.

❮ ❮ ❮ Try the Champagne cocktail **Mayfair Fizz No. 2** for its complex combination of flavors.

sweet & creamy

S weet and creamy flavors bring a sense of well-being to the psyche. There's nothing to match rolling your tongue around your mouth to capture every last drop of pleasure. Each of the flavors in this section—chocolate, cream, and honey—offers rich, multilayered pleasures when combined in a cocktail with compatible ingredients.

Cream gives a luxurious body to a cocktail. Heavy (double) cream is used for many recipes and is an ingredient in a growing number of liqueurs. Baileys Original Irish Cream is the best-known of these. To sip a glass of Baileys is to experience something unique. Made with all-natural ingredients (fresh dairy cream, a triple-distilled whiskey, and a natural cocoa extract from Belgium), Baileys is the world's best-selling liqueur.

Pure honey has a piquant sweetness of its own and is also a natural product with health benefits. You can tailor honey-based cocktails to your own taste by choosing honey from a specific plant source, whose flavor will be present in the honey. Clover honey has a pure, neutral flavor, for instance, whereas chestnut honey has a heavy, nutty tone, and Mediterranean honeys can be very herbaceous.

Chocolate, when infused in spirits, has an entire range of flavors from earthy to fruity (depending on whether it is dark, milk, or white). A high dairy content (less cocoa solids) means mellower milky and caramel flavors. The cocoa should have a hint of bitterness, but only a hint. In dark chocolate, you might discover cocoa, hints of pineapple, banana, passion fruit, vanilla, cinnamon, or combinations of these flavors.

Chocolate mixes well with spirits, and in particular whiskey, bourbon, Armagnac, and Cognac. Rum can also provide a good spirit base for a smooth, chocolate-flavored cocktail. In a cocktail, chocolate makes its mark strongly with a sweet statement, but a textural layer also declares its presence.

Chocolate liqueurs come in dark, milk, and white chocolate flavors, and many incorporate cream as well. The ingredient crème de cacao is another cocoa liqueur, and it is available in white and dark varieties, referring to its color rather than the type of chocolate. *Crème* refers to its thick texture; it contains no actual cream.

My advice: Too much of even a high-quality chocolate flavor can be too much of a good thing, so follow the amounts in the recipe instructions carefully.

chocolate

Depending on the percentage of cocoa solids and the origin of the chocolate you buy, flavors range from slightly bitter to sweet and creamy, with hints of floral, fruity, or spicy finishing notes. In spirits, dark chocolate lends an earthy note and white chocolate is smooth and sweet.

Aztec Gift

1 oz / 3 cl	bourbon
⅔ oz / 2 cl	dark chocolate liqueur
⅓ oz / 1 cl	Port
⅓ oz / 1 cl	Frangelico
½ oz / 1.5 cl	blueberry juice

Combine the ingredients in a shaker with ice and shake. Strain into a chilled cocktail glass.

Caribbean Mozart

½ oz / 1.5 cl	rum
1¾ oz / 5 cl	white chocolate liqueur
½ oz / 1.5 cl	coconut syrup (page 21)
GARNISH	small wedge of fresh pineapple

Combine the ingredients in a mixing glass with ice and stir. Pour into a liqueur glass. Add the garnish.

Chocolate Affair

1 oz / 3 cl	chocolate liqueur
½ oz / 1.5 cl	Tia Maria
½ oz / 1.5 cl	Cognac
½ oz / 1.5 cl	amaretto
⅔ oz / 2 cl	heavy (double) cream
GARNISH	grated chocolate

Combine the ingredients in a shaker with ice and shake. Strain into a chilled cocktail glass and add the garnish.

Chocolate Colada

1 oz / 3 cl	light rum
1¾ oz / 5 cl	white chocolate liqueur
1 oz / 3 cl	coconut syrup (page 21)
½ oz / 1.5 cl	heavy (double) cream
3 oz / 9 cl	pineapple juice
GARNISH	grated chocolate

Combine the ingredients in a shaker with ice and shake. Strain into a colada glass filled with crushed ice. Add the garnish.

Chocolate Martini

2 oz / 6 cl	vodka
1 oz / 3 cl	white chocolate liqueur
	cocoa powder
	wedge of orange

Use the cocoa and the wedge of orange to crust a chilled cocktail glass (see page 14). Combine the ingredients in a shaker with ice and shake. Strain into the prepared glass.

Chocolate Rum

1 oz / 3 cl	light rum
1 tsp	151 proof rum
1 oz / 3 cl	white crème de cacao
½ oz / 1.5 cl	white crème de menthe
1 tbsp	heavy (double) cream

Combine the ingredients in a shaker with ice and shake. Strain into an old-fashioned glass filled with ice cubes. Stir.

Easter-tini

1⅔ oz / 5 cl	vodka
⅔ oz / 2 cl	white crème de cacao
⅓ oz / 1 cl	Cointreau
dash	Sambuca
GARNISH	mini chocolate egg

Combine the ingredients in a shaker with ice and shake. Strain into a cocktail glass and add the garnish.

Mulata

1½ oz / 4.5 cl	white rum
⅔ oz / 2 cl	brown crème de cacao
⅔ oz / 2 cl	fresh lime juice
⅓ oz / 1 cl	simple syrup (page 20)
GARNISH	grated chocolate

Combine the ingredients in a shaker with ice and shake. Strain into a chilled cocktail glass and add the garnish.

cream

Good cream has the delicate sweetness of milk and a thickness that can be felt, similar to, say, a very soft cream cheese. In drinks, the thickness of cream, whether in pure form or in a cream-based liqueur, lends texture to a sophisticated cocktail with all the appeal of an ice-cream dessert.

Baileys Banana Colada

2 oz / 6 cl	Baileys Irish Cream
1 oz / 3 cl	Parrot Bay rum
1	banana
GARNISH	slice of banana

Combine the ingredients in a blender with crushed ice and blend until smooth. Pour into a highball filled with ice. Add the garnish. Serve with a straw.

Brandy Alexander

1 oz / 3 cl	Cognac
1 oz / 3 cl	brown crème de cacao
1 oz / 3 cl	heavy (double) cream
GARNISH	freshly grated nutmeg

Combine the ingredients in a shaker with ice and shake. Strain into a cocktail glass. Grate the nutmeg over the drink.

Cupid's Corner

1 oz / 3 cl	Cognac
1 oz / 3 cl	Chambord liqueur
1 oz / 3 cl	heavy (double) cream
dash	grenadine

Combine the ingredients in a shaker with ice and shake. Strain into a chilled cocktail glass.

Flip My Lid

1 oz / 3 cl	dark rum
½ oz / 1.5 cl	Port
½ oz / 1.5 cl	Pisang Ambon liqueur
1 oz / 3 cl	heavy (double) cream
⅓ oz / 1 cl	honey syrup (page 22)
1	pasteurized egg yolk

Combine the ingredients in a shaker with ice and shake. Strain into a chilled cocktail glass.

Golden Cadillac

1 oz / 3 cl	white crème de cacao
⅔ oz / 2 cl	Galliano liqueur
1 oz / 3 cl	heavy (double) cream

Combine the ingredients in a shaker with ice and shake. Strain into a chilled cocktail glass.

Grasshopper

1 oz / 3 cl	green crème de menthe
1 oz / 3 cl	white crème de cacao
1 oz / 3 cl	heavy (double) cream

Combine the ingredients in a shaker with ice and shake. Strain into a chilled cocktail glass.

Sloe Gin Flip

1 oz / 3 cl	sloe gin
2 tbsps	light cream
1 tsp	confectioner's (powdered) sugar
1	pasteurized egg
GARNISH	freshly grated nutmeg

Combine the ingredients in a shaker with ice and shake. Strain into an old-fashioned glass filled with ice. Grate the nutmeg over the drink.

Snow Cream

2 oz / 6 cl	Baileys Irish Cream
½ oz / 1.5 cl	Chambord liqueur
dash	grenadine

Combine the ingredients in a shaker with ice and shake. Strain into a chilled cocktail glass.

The **Grasshopper** is both sweet and creamy with a great mint finish. ❯ ❯ ❯

honey

Honey comes in many exotic flavors, depending on the flowers from which it originates. The basic taste is sweet, but the underlying aromas can be earthy, floral, fruity, or nutty.

Bee's Knees

2 oz / 6 cl	gin
¾ oz / 2.5 cl	honey syrup (page 22)
½ oz / 1.5 cl	fresh lemon juice

GARNISH   lemon spiral

Combine the ingredients in a shaker with ice and shake. Strain into a chilled Champagne coupe and add the garnish.

Honey Bee

2 oz / 6 cl	dark rum
¾ oz / 2.5 cl	honey syrup (page 22)
½ oz / 1.5 cl	fresh lemon juice

GARNISH   twist of lemon

Combine the ingredients in a shaker with ice and shake. Strain into a chilled Champagne coupe and add the garnish.

Chile & Honey Cocktail

⅔ oz / 5 cl	manuka honey vodka
half	lime
1	kaffir lime leaf
2	small slices of chile
½ oz / 1.5 cl	Jägermeister
⅓ oz / 1 cl	elderflower water
½ oz / 1.5 cl	honey syrup (page 22)

GARNISH   kaffir lime leaves

Muddle the kaffir lime leaf with the chile in the bottom of a shaker. Add ice and remaining ingredients and shake. Double-strain into a chilled cocktail glass. Add the garnish to the side of the glass.

Honeysuckle Cocktail

1⅔ oz / 5 cl	light rum
⅔ oz / 2 cl	fresh lime juice
⅔ oz / 2 cl	honey syrup (page 22)

Combine the ingredients in a shaker with ice and shake. Strain into a chilled cocktail glass.

Honeysuckle Daiquiri

2 oz / 6 cl	light rum
1 oz / 3 cl	honey syrup (page 22)
1 oz / 3 cl	fresh lemon juice
1 oz / 3 cl	fresh orange juice

GARNISH   mint leaf

Combine the ingredients in a shaker with ice and shake. Strain into a chilled cocktail glass. Add the garnish.

Honey-tini

2 oz / 6 cl	honey vodka
½ oz / 1.5 cl	apple juice
GARNISH	apple fan (see page 15)

Combine the ingredients in a shaker with ice and shake. Strain into a chilled cocktail glass. Add the garnish.

Honey Toddy

2 oz / 6 cl	Scotch
1 oz / 3 cl	clear honey
½ oz / 1.5 cl	fresh lemon juice
2 pieces	honeycomb
1 oz / 3 cl	water
GARNISH	twist of lemon, small piece of honeycomb

Combine the ingredients in a saucepan over low heat and warm them gently. Pour into a heatproof glass. Add the garnish.

Honey, Trust Me!

2 oz / 6 cl	honey vodka
½ oz / 1.5 cl	brown crème de cacao
½ oz / 1.5 cl	limoncello
1 oz / 3 cl	heavy (double) cream
GARNISH	grated lemon zest

Combine the ingredients in a shaker with ice and shake. Strain into a chilled cocktail glass. Grate the zest over the top.

unusual flavors

There are rare moments when an ingredient usually regarded as a food can be adapted for a cocktail. The skill lies in selecting something to complement and enhance the food ingredient.

I was in a restaurant bar in Moscow eating smoked salmon when the owner of the restaurant asked me to create a cocktail for his bar. The flavor of the smoked salmon and its oily texture were an inspiration to me, and the resulting cocktail recipe, called Sassy Salmon, is on page 167.

Other unusual ingredients used to flavor cocktails include balsamic vinegar, garlic, popcorn, and truffle—an eclectic collection if ever there was one!

When using any of these unusual flavors, the trick is to make sure you select the freshest kind available so the full spectrum of its flavor comes through. If the item is fresh, you need only use a small amount of it. Dried or preserved versions are not as full of flavor as the fresh item.

True balsamic vinegar is made from the concentrated juice of northern Italian grapes. During the aging of an Italian traditional balsamic the vinegar is shifted from one type of wood barrel to the next. The cherry, chestnut, oak, mulberry, and other barrels all leave their imprint on the flavor of the vinegar. This brings an unbelievable concentration of sweet-sour flavor in a dense, brown-black vinegar with hints of berries, grapes, and vanilla. Balsamic vinegar goes well with fresh, sweet strawberries and sweet liqueurs. Look for Italian balsamics with the word *Tradizionale* on the label for the true product—there are many commercial imitations on the shelves.

Garlic has a sweet pungency that is released when the skin is peeled away and the garlic clove is sliced open. My advice is to prepare the garlic not in advance, but at the moment it is required.

As for the unique, woody flavor of the truffle, it can only be seen in the finest company, and Champagne fits that bill. Fresh truffles are best for an infusion. Some of the recipes in this book call for truffle paste, but some bartenders will use truffle oil.

Follow the recipes exactly and you will learn about balance and the harmony of flavors that may have originally surprised you.

For the discerning, **Maestro** offers a challenging combination of flavors. ❯ ❯ ❯

balsamic vinegar

The white, sugary Trebbiano grapes grown in northern Italy near Modena provide the base of true balsamic vinegars, which are rich, sweet, and subtly woody.

Balsamic Twist

1⅓ oz / 4 cl	grappa
⅔ oz / 2 cl	Mandarine Napoleon liqueur
⅓ oz / 1 cl	marascino liqueur
2 tsps	aged balsamic vinegar
GARNISH	twist of orange

Combine the ingredients in a shaker with ice and shake. Strain into a chilled cocktail glass. Add the garnish.

Intrigue

1⅔ oz / 5 cl	Cognac
½ oz / 1.5 cl	white crème de cacao
½ oz / 1.5 cl	dry white wine
⅔ oz / 2 cl	raspberry puree
2 tsps	balsamic vinegar
dash	honey syrup (page 22)
GARNISH	raspberry, mint leaves

Combine the ingredients in a shaker with ice and shake. Strain into a chilled cocktail glass. Add the garnish.

Maestro

1⅓ oz / 4 cl	vodka
⅔ oz / 2 cl	crème de fraise
2 dashes	fresh lime juice
2 dashes	maple syrup
2 dashes	balsamic vinegar
GARNISH	half a strawberry

Combine the ingredients in a shaker with ice and shake. Strain into a chilled cocktail glass. Add the half a strawberry on the rim of the glass.

Thanksgiving Cocktail

2 oz / 6 cl	bourbon
1 oz / 3 cl	cranberry juice
½ oz / 1.5 cl	agave syrup
⅓ oz / 1 cl	aged balsamic vinegar
GARNISH	string of red currants

Combine the ingredients in a shaker with ice and shake. Strain into a chilled cocktail glass. Add the garnish across the top of the glass.

fish

The flavor of fish is unexpected in a cocktail, but the natural oils and saltiness of fish marry well with citrus and spice.

Dried Crab Cocktail

1⅓ oz / 4 cl	gin
⅔ oz / 2 cl	dry sherry
⅔ oz / 2 cl	Grand Marnier
⅓ oz / 1 cl	fresh lemon juice
1 tsp	honey
1	thin slice of chile
1	tamago kani (Japanese dried crab)
GARNISH	tamago kani

Muddle the crab in the bottom of a shaker. Add ice and the remaining ingredients and shake. Double-strain into a chilled cocktail glass. Serve with a dried crab on the side.

Fish Shot

1 oz / 3 cl	vodka
1½ oz / 4.5 cl	cold fish consommé
dash	soy sauce
twist	freshly ground black pepper
GARNISH	twist of freshly ground black pepper

Combine the ingredients in a shaker with ice and shake. Strain into a shot glass and add the garnish.

Sassy Salmon

1⅔ oz / 5 cl	vodka
⅔ oz / 2 cl	dry white wine
⅔ oz / 2 cl	fresh lemon juice
1	piece smoked salmon two fingers wide
1	small piece fresh dill
2	thin slices chile
GARNISH	sprig of dill

Gently muddle the smoked salmon, dill, and chile with the lemon juice in the bottom of a shaker. Add ice and the remaining ingredients and shake. Strain into a cocktail glass. Add the garnish.

garlic

Here's a flavor you don't expect in a cocktail. Garlic provides a spicy, earthy foil to sweet ingredients and pairs well with equally spicy ginger flavors.

popcorn

Warm and toasty is probably the best way to describe the flavor of our favorite snack. I have included this for its fun factor.

Garlic Affair

1 oz / 3 cl	Cognac
½ oz / 1.5 cl	apricot brandy
½ oz / 1.5 cl	fresh lemon juice
	ginger beer
	garlic clove
GARNISH	wedge of lime

Gently muddle the garlic in the bottom of a shaker. Add ice and all the remaining ingredients except the ginger beer and shake. Strain into a highball filled with ice. Top up with ginger beer and stir. Add the garnish.

At the Movies

2 oz / 6 cl	light rum
5 oz / 15 cl	vanilla syrup (page 24)
1 cup	air-popped popcorn (set aside a few piece for garnish)
1	egg white
	club soda
GARNISH	popcorn

Heat the vanilla syrup in a small saucepan over low heat. Stir in the popcorn and simmer gently until the syrup turns light gold in color and begins to caramelize. Remove from the heat and let cool. Gently strain off the popcorn and discard, reserving the syrup.

Combine the rum, ½ oz/1.5 cl reserved syrup, and the egg white in a shaker with ice and shake. Strain into a highball filled with ice. Top up with club soda and stir. Serve with a straw and a few pieces of dry popcorn on top of the drink.

truffle

Truffles are prized for their unique musky flavor and aroma, regardless of whether they are white or black. Black truffles are usually used in cooking and making Martinis.

Truffle and Pear Cocktail

1½ oz / 4.5 cl	truffle vodka* (see below)
½ oz / 1.5 cl	pear brandy
1 oz / 3 cl	pear puree
1 spritz	truffle essence
GARNISH	wedge of pear

Combine all the ingredients except the truffle essence in a shaker with ice and shake. Strain into a chilled cocktail glass and spray the truffle essence on top. Add the garnish.

Truffle Margarita

2 oz / 6 cl	truffle tequila* (see below)
½ oz / 1.5 cl	fresh yuzu juice
½ oz / 1.5 cl	fresh lime juice
½ oz / 1.5 cl	agave syrup
	Hawaiian black salt
	wedge of lime

Use the Hawaiian black salt and the wedge of lime to crust a Champagne coupe (see page 14). Combine the ingredients in a shaker with ice and shake. Strain into the prepared glass.

*To infuse the vodka or tequila: clean a small black truffle. Cut it in half and add to a bottle of vodka or tequila. Let the flavor develop for at least 1 week at room temperature (longer for a more intense flavor). Fine strain into a clean bottle and use as needed.

Truffle Martini

1 bottle / 75 cl	vodka
1⅔ oz / 5 cl	grappa
1	whole black truffle, thinly sliced
2 or 3	fresh ginger slices
	Champagne

Place the sliced truffle in the vodka. Add the ginger and grappa. With the cap on, shake the bottle. Place in the freezer for one week to infuse the flavors. To make one cocktail: Pour 2 ounces of the vodka into a chilled cocktail glass. Top up with Champagne and stir.

White Chocolate Truffle Martini

1½ oz / 4.5 cl	vodka
½ oz / 1.5 cl	grappa di moscato
⅔ oz / 2 cl	white chocolate liqueur
⅔ oz / 2 cl	heavy (double) cream
¼ tsp	white truffle paste
GARNISH	thin slice of truffle

Combine the ingredients in a shaker with ice and shake. Strain into a chilled cocktail glass and add the garnish.

vegetables

Who would have thought rhubarb and grapefruit juice would go together with a measure of English gin? Or horseradish vodka with tangerine and fresh lemon juice? The recipes in this section will open your mind as to what you can achieve with a little imagination, flair, and confidence.

The idea of vegetable juice in a nonalcoholic cocktail is not new, whereas the idea of beet juice with chilled vodka is certainly an interesting one. Both the beet and the fleshy, crisp, sweet bell pepper (capsicum) complement a cocktail, offering color as well as flavor.

The recent predilection for cocktails made with fresh vegetables is part of a trend for a healthier lifestyle without saying no to alcohol. Vodka, light rum, silver tequila, and gin are enlivened by vegetable juices in a delicious way.

Carrot, cucumber, and rhubarb each have a light flavor and as such are good mixers in small quantities. Carrot juice is already a popular mainstream drink. When you think of mixing it, remember that the flavor of carrot has an affinity for honey, raisins, cinnamon, and nutmeg, as well as cream. Carrot juice is the perfect cocktail ingredient, at home with other flavors without dominating.

Cucumber has an herbaceous, sweet, grassy flavor. Put it together with mint, vinegar, chile, lemon, and ginger and it will hold its own.

Rhubarb juice is sweet and offers tannin and acidity, and what a lovely color it imparts to a cocktail!

Which leaves the matter of horseradish vodka. Its hot, peppery flavor is an acquired taste, but then again, it all depends upon the other flavors used to balance its pungency.

As always, look for the freshest vegetables to obtain the freshest flavors.

asparagus

This is a spring vegetable, highly nutritious, with an earthy flavor. Only the tips of tender young spears of green asparagus should be used; thicker specimens will be too tough and woody.

Bloody Asparagus

1½ oz / 4.5 cl	vodka
5 oz / 15 cl	tomato juice
¾ oz / 2.5 cl	fresh lemon juice
3 dashes	Worcestershire sauce
2 dashes	Tabasco
pinch	salt
twist	fresh ground black pepper
GARNISH	fresh asparagus spear

Muddle the asparagus in the bottom of the shaker. Add the remaining ingredients and ice and shake. Double-strain into a highball filled with ice. Garnish with a spear of asparagus cut in half across.

Note: If you want a stronger flavor of asparagus, increase the amount.

Market Garden

1⅔ oz / 5 cl	white rum
⅔ oz / 2 cl	Falernum
⅔ oz / 2 cl	pear puree
¾ oz / 2.5 cl	fresh lime juice
1 tsp	clear honey
1	fresh asparagus tip
GARNISH	asparagus spear

Muddle the asparagus in the bottom of a shaker. Add ice and the remaining ingredients and shake. Double-strain into a Champagne coupe. Slit the asparagus spear and place it on the rim of the glass.

Mexican Spring

1⅔ oz / 5 cl	reposado tequila
½ oz / 1.5 cl	Cointreau
½ oz / 1.5 cl	fresh lime juice
1 tsp	agave syrup
1	fresh asparagus tip
1	thin slice of fresh fennel
GARNISH	thin slice of asparagus

Muddle the vegetables with the agave syrup in the bottom of a shaker. Add ice and the remaining ingredients and shake. Double-strain into a chilled cocktail glass and add the garnish.

beet

Beets have an intense, sweet, earthy flavor when cooked.
For these recipes, beets were handled in various ways: small beets
were roasted and cooled, then either pureed until smooth
or muddled, or the beets were pickled, then muddled.

Beet-ini

1½ oz / 4.5 cl	vodka
½ oz / 1.5 cl	crème de fraise des bois
1 oz / 3 cl	fresh beet puree
1 oz / 3 cl	cranberry juice
1 tsp	vanilla sugar
GARNISH	two chive "straws"

Combine the ingredients in a shaker with ice
and shake. Strain into a chilled cocktail glass.
Add the garnish.

Elit Kiss

1⅔ oz / 5 cl	Stoli Elit
½ oz / 1.5 cl	maraschino liqueur
⅓ oz / 1 cl	fresh lime juice
3 dashes	orange bitters
2	slices of pickled beet plus 1 tsp of the juice
GARNISH	sprig of dill, thin slice of heart-shaped beet

Gently muddle the beet in the bottom of a
shaker. Add ice and the remaining ingredients
and shake. Double-strain into a chilled cocktail glass and add the garnish.

Russian Experience

2 oz / 6 cl	vodka
dash	fresh lemon juice
half	medium-size cooked beet
pinch	cracked black pepper
pinch	salt
2	thin slices cucumber
GARNISH	sprig of dill, lemongrass

Muddle the beet, lemon juice, and cucumber
in the bottom of a shaker. Add ice and the
remaining ingredients and shake. Strain into a
chilled cocktail glass. Add the garnish.

Elit Kiss offers grown-up flavor
and stunning color. ❯ ❯ ❯

bell pepper

Also known as capsicum, this fleshy, sweet vegetable
simply bursts with juicy flavor. Cut bell peppers into strips
when muddling them in the bottom of a shaker.
This releases the flavor better.

Rattle and Hum

1 oz / 3 cl	silver tequila
½ oz / 1.5 cl	Passoa
⅓ oz / 1 cl	Van Der Hum
½ oz / 1.5 cl	honey syrup (page 22)
½ oz / 1.5 cl	fresh lime juice
⅔ oz / 2 cl	guava juice
5	small pieces of yellow bell pepper
GARNISH	2 thin slices of yellow pepper, sprig of mint

Muddle the pepper in the bottom of a shaker.
Add ice and the remaining ingredients and
shake. Strain into a chilled wine glass filled
with crushed ice. Lay the garnish on top of
the drink.

Yellow Lamborghini

1⅔ oz / 5 cl	frozen vodka
⅔ oz / 2 cl	Galliano liqueur
2 dashes	lemon bitters
2	thin slices yellow bell pepper
GARNISH	fine strips of yellow pepper

Gently muddle the pepper in the bottom
of a mixing glass. Add ice and the remaining
ingredients and stir. Strain into a chilled
cocktail glass and add the garnish.

‹ ‹ ‹ Yellow bell peppers are
the designated garnish for the
cocktail **Rattle and Hum**.

carrot

Carrots contain more vitamin A than any other vegetable. A sweet and earthy flavor dominates the fresh juice. Look for medium-size carrots because large ones can have an unappetizing woody center.

Carrot Zest

2 oz / 6 cl	vodka
2 oz / 6 cl	carrot juice
2 oz / 6 cl	tomato juice
1 tsp	clear honey
1 oz / 3 cl	fresh lemon juice
dash	Worcestershire sauce
2 or 3	thin slices fresh ginger
GARNISH	red and yellow cherry tomatoes, cut in half; basil leaf

Muddle the ginger in the bottom of a shaker. Add ice and the remaining ingredients and shake. Pour into a highball, letting the ice fall into the glass. Add the garnish on a cocktail stick.

Life Saver

2 oz / 6 cl	vodka
3 oz / 9 cl	carrot juice
1 oz / 3 cl	apple juice
2	thin slices fresh ginger
GARNISH	thin wedge of lime

Combine the ingredients in a shaker with ice and shake. Strain into a highball filled with ice. Slit the lime and place it on the rim of the glass.

Vitamin Hit

1⅔ oz / 5 cl	vodka
⅔ oz / 2 cl	elderflower liqueur
2 oz / 6 cl	carrot juice
1 oz / 3 cl	Granny Smith apple juice
1 oz / 3 cl	fresh lime juice
2	thin slices fresh ginger
GARNISH	slice of dried pineapple, sprig of mint, and a cherry

Muddle the ginger in the bottom of a shaker. Add ice and the remaining ingredients and shake. Strain into a highball filled with ice. Add the garnish. Serve with a straw.

❮ ❮ ❮ **Vitamin Hit**—it's not only good for you, it tastes good too.

cucumber

The younger, small, and slender cucumbers are usually sweeter than the larger versions. Cucumbers with waxed skins require peeling; those with seeds need the seeds removed. A good cucumber will have a fresh, vegetal flavor.

C C Cooler

2 oz / 6 cl	Hendrick's gin
1 oz / 3 cl	apple juice
1 oz / 3 cl	cranberry juice
quarter	small cucumber, diced
3	mint leaves
GARNISH	slice of cucumber

Muddle the cucumber and mint in the bottom of a shaker. Add ice and the remaining ingredients and shake hard to bruise the mint. Double-strain into a highball filled with crushed ice. Add the garnish. Serve with a straw.

Cucumber Martini

2 oz / 6 cl	vodka
quarter	small cucumber, diced
dash	simple syrup (page 20)
GARNISH	cucumber spiral

Muddle the cucumber in the bottom of a shaker. Add ice and the remaining ingredients and shake. Double-strain into a chilled cocktail glass. Add the garnish.

Cool Cucumber

1½ oz / 4.5 cl	gin
dash	Campari
1 oz / 3 cl	fresh orange juice
dash	simple syrup (page 20)
3	slices cucumber
GARNISH	slice of cucumber

Muddle the cucumber in the bottom of a shaker. Add ice and the remaining ingredients and shake. Double-strain into a chilled cocktail glass. Add the garnish.

horseradish

An unusual flavor to find in a cocktail, horseradish is spicy on the tongue, with hints of pepper in the finish. All the recipes here use horseradish-flavored spirits.

Horseradish Margarita

1½ oz / 4.5 cl	horseradish-infused tequila*
½ oz / 1.5 cl	Cointreau
¾ oz / 2 cl	fresh lime juice
½ oz / 1.5 cl	fresh pomegranate juice
dash	simple syrup (see page 20)
GARNISH	twist of lime

Combine the ingredients in a shaker with ice and shake. Strain into an old-fashioned glass filled with ice. Add the garnish.

*Place ⅓ cup fresh horseradish, peeled and chopped, into 1 cup of silver tequila. Stir and let sit for 24 hours.

Hummer

1⅓ oz / 4 cl	horseradish vodka
⅔ oz / 2 cl	Cointreau
1 oz / 3 cl	carrot juice
1⅔ oz / 5 cl	fresh apple juice
2 dashes	ginger puree

Combine the ingredients in a shaker with ice and shake. Strain into a chilled cocktail glass.

Hot Voodoo Love

1½ oz / 4.5 cl	horseradish vodka
½ oz / 1.5 cl	sweet vermouth
1 oz / 3 cl	fresh lemon juice
½ oz / 1.5 cl	tangerine juice
½ oz / 1.5 cl	simple syrup (page 20)
dash	Angostura bitters
GARNISH	orange twist

Combine the ingredients in a shaker with ice and shake. Strain into a chilled cocktail glass. Add the garnish.

rhubarb

In its raw state, rhubarb is sour and unappetizing, but when it is stewed with sugar and strained, the resulting rhubarb juice is an exotic addition to any cocktail. Try gin, apple, or orange with it.

Rhubarb Cosmo

1⅓ oz / 4 cl	vodka
½ oz / 1.5 cl	triple sec or Cointreau
⅔ oz / 2 cl	fresh rhubarb juice
½ oz / 1.5 cl	fresh lime juice

Combine the ingredients in a shaker with ice and shake. Strain into a chilled cocktail glass.

Rhuby

1⅔ oz / 5 cl	cachaça
1 oz / 3 cl	rhubarb syrup
⅔ oz / 2 cl	fresh lime juice
GARNISH	slice of star fruit, peeled wedge of dragon fruit

Combine the ingredients in a shaker with ice and shake. Strain into a chilled cocktail glass. Slit the dragon fruit and star fruit and place them on the rim of the glass.

Spring Tao

1⅔ oz / 5 cl	Hendrick's gin
1 oz / 3 cl	pink grapefruit juice
dash	simple syrup (page 20)
4	small pieces fresh rhubarb
GARNISH	rhubarb stick

Muddle the rhubarb with the simple syrup in the bottom of a shaker. Add ice and the remaining ingredients and shake. Strain through a tea strainer into an old-fashioned glass filled with ice. Add the garnish.

zucchini

A tender young zucchini will add a surprisingly delicate, light, fresh flavor to a cocktail. Look for small, firm, fresh specimens and do not peel them, as it is the skin that gives the drink its color.

Green Hombre

1²/₃ oz / 5 cl	reposado tequila
¹/₃ oz / 1 cl	green Chartreuse
²/₃ oz / 2 cl	fresh lime juice
¹/₃ oz / 1 cl	agave syrup
3	wedges zucchini
	pinch of salt

Muddle the zucchini and the salt in the bottom of a shaker. Add ice and the remaining ingredients and shake. Double-strain into a chilled Champagne coupe.

Zucchini Smoothie *(nonalcoholic)*

1	zucchini, peeled and chopped
1	apple, peeled, cored, and chopped
1	banana, peeled and chopped
4 oz / 2 cl	water

Combine the ingredients in a blender with 1 scoop of crushed ice and blend until smooth and creamy. Pour into a highball and serve with a straw.

Zucchini-tini

1¹/₃ oz / 4 cl	sake
²/₃ oz / 2 cl	gin
½ oz / 1.5 cl	zucchini water*
½ oz / 1.5 cl	simple syrup (page 20)
GARNISH	thin slice of zucchini

Combine the ingredients in a shaker with ice and shake. Strain into a chilled cocktail glass and add the garnish.

*To make zucchini water: Grate a zucchini into a fine-mesh sieve placed over a bowl. Sprinkle the zucchini with a pinch of salt and leave it for 15 minutes. Press the zucchini to extract as much water as possible.

wine
flavors

hampagne is crafted primarily from Chardonnay, Pinot Noir, and Pinot Meunier, either alone or in blends. The purple Pinot Noir grape has a colorless, sugary juice that gives body and long life to the wine, while the small Chardonnay grape contributes the perfume. Usually of a light straw color (but sometimes rosé) with small bubbles, Champagne differs in flavor from house to house and from vintage to vintage. For cocktail-making, a less expensive Champagne is fine, although it shouldn't be bottom of the line. The affordable Cava and Crémant de Bourgogne, made using the same traditional method as in Champagne, may be substituted, but other sparkling wines such as Prosecco lack Champagne's depth of flavor.

Vermouth is an aromatized, fortified wine. Its name is derived from the German *Wermut* (wormwood), an herb that was added to wine for medicinal purposes as far back as 78 AD. Traditionally, Italians made sweeter, heavier vermouths, and the French made lighter, drier ones. Now both countries produce all types, using a combination of ingredients such as quinine, coriander, juniper, and orange peel.

Wine is full of flavors that can subtly influence a cocktail. In general, choose a dry wine that you enjoy drinking on its own for cocktail-making. For white wines, Sauvignon Blanc has fresh, gooseberry or tropical fruit flavors, dry Riesling offers hints of green apple, and Chardonnay has luscious honeysuckle and peach flavors with a smoky oak aroma. For red wines, try Cabernet, with its black currant and raspberry flavors, or Shiraz, which might have blackberry, plum, chocolate, and spice aromas.

With its magnificent color and fullness,
Bunny Bubbles truly shines. ❯ ❯ ❯

champagne

A fine Champagne is complex, with words like
delicate green apple, rich, creamy, toasty, crisp, slightly tart,
floral, and perfumed used to describe its unique flavor.

Bunny Bubbles

½ oz / 1.5 cl	Bénédictine
1 oz / 3 cl	fresh raspberry puree
½ oz / 1.5 cl	pomegranate juice
	Champagne
GARNISH	2 raspberries, mint leaf

Combine all the ingredients except the
Champagne in a shaker with ice and shake.
Strain into an Art-Deco Champagne coupe.
Rinse the shaker with Champagne, add it
to the drink, and stir. Add the garnish on a
cocktail stick.

Champagne Cocktail

½ oz / 1.5 cl	Cognac
1	white sugar cube
2 drops	Angostura bitters
	Champagne
GARNISH	quarter slice of orange, maraschino cherry (optional)

Place the sugar in the bottom of a Champagne
flute and pour the drops of Angostura over
it. Add the Cognac. Top up with Champagne.
Pour the Champagne very slowly, to prevent
it from bubbling over. Add the garnish.

Champagne Tropicale

1 oz / 3 cl	maraschino liqueur
1⅓ oz / 4 cl	mango puree
	Champagne
GARNISH	maraschino cherry

Pour the liqueur and puree into a mixing
glass. Add the Champagne and stir gently
to combine the two. Pour into a Champagne
flute and add the garnish.

Exotic flavors make the Champagne
cocktails **Melon Fizz** (foreground) and
Pussycat deliciously desirable. ❯ ❯ ❯

Le Grand Cognac

1 oz / 3 cl	Cognac
6	black grapes
dash	vanilla syrup (page 24)
	Champagne

Muddle the grapes in the bottom of an old-fashioned glass. Add the Cognac and the syrup and stir. Fill with crushed ice and top up with Champagne. Stir gently.

Melon Fizz

½ oz / 1.5 cl	Cointreau
dash	simple syrup (page 20)
quarter	cantaloupe, diced
	Champagne
GARNISH	thin slice of melon

Combine all the ingredients except the Champagne in a blender with a handful of crushed ice and blend until smooth. Double-strain into a Champagne coupe. Top up with Champagne and stir. Slit the melon and place it on the rim of the glass.

Metropolis II

1 oz / 3 cl	vodka
1 oz / 3 cl	crème de framboise
	Champagne

Combine the vodka and crème de framboise in a shaker with ice and shake. Strain into a Champagne coupe. Top up with Champagne and stir.

Pussycat

½ oz / 1.5 cl	Parfait Amour
½ oz / 1.5 cl	crème de fraise
⅔ oz / 2 cl	raspberry puree
	Champagne
GARNISH	strawberry fan (page 15)

Combine all the ingredients except the Champagne in a shaker with ice and shake. Strain into a chilled Champagne flute. Top up with Champagne. Add the garnish.

vermouth

The four styles of vermouth range from dry to sweet: extra dry, bianco/
white, sweet/red, and rosé. French vermouths are sweet or dry, with
a spicy aroma. Italian vermouths have a wider flavor base.

Alfonso XIII

1½ oz / 4.5 cl	dry sherry
1½ oz / 4.5 cl	red Dubonnet
slice	orange dusted with
	cinnamon
GARNISH	orange peel

Muddle the orange slice with the sherry
in the bottom of a shaker. Add ice and the
Dubonnet and shake. Strain into a chilled
cocktail glass. Use a lighter or match to lightly
flame the outside of the orange peel and
drop it into the drink.

Aviator

⅔ oz / 2 cl	dry vermouth
⅔ oz / 2 cl	sweet vermouth
⅔ oz / 2 cl	red Dubonnet
⅔ oz / 2 cl	gin
GARNISH	twist of lemon

Combine the ingredients in a mixing glass
with ice and stir. Strain into a chilled cocktail
glass. Add the garnish.

Italian White Sangria *serves 6*

1 bottle / 75 cl	dry vermouth
8 oz / 24 cl	orange liqueur
8 oz / 24 cl	fresh orange juice
2 oz / 6 cl	fresh lemon juice
½ cup	superfine (caster) sugar
1 each	orange, lemon, lime, and
	apple, thinly sliced
	sparkling mineral water

Combine the sugar, vermouth, liqueur, and
orange and lemon juices in a punch bowl
or large pitcher and stir until the sugar is
dissolved. Chill until ready to serve. Stir in the
fruit and sparkling water. Add ice at the last
moment.

wine

Whether red or white, it is best to select a dry wine for cocktail-making unless a recipe requests a sweet one, such as Port. See page 182 for suggestions.

Claret Cobbler

2 oz / 6 cl	red Bordeaux (claret)
1 oz / 3 cl	vodka
½ oz / 1.5 cl	crème de framboise
slice	lemon
wedge	orange
GARNISH	wedge of lime, slice of lemon

Muddle the fruit in the bottom of a shaker. Add ice and the remaining ingredients and shake. Strain into a wine glass or small goblet filled with ice. Add the garnish.

Code Red

1 oz / 3 cl	gin
½ oz / 1.5 cl	limoncello
⅔ oz / 2 cl	red wine
⅓ oz / 1 cl	fresh lime juice
2 tsps	simple syrup (page 20)

Combine all ingredients except the red wine in a shaker with ice and shake. Strain into a chilled cocktail glass. Float the red wine over the top.

Italian Spritzer

1½ oz / 4.5 cl	Aperol
3 oz / 9 cl	Prosecco
GARNISH	slice of orange

Combine the Aperol and the Prosecco in a large chilled wine glass filled with ice and stir. Add the garnish.

Jamaican Sangria

1⅓ oz / 4 cl	Jamaican rum
1 oz / 3 cl	red wine
½ oz / 1.5 cl	apricot brandy
½ oz / 1.5 cl	framboise liqueur
1⅔ oz / 5 cl	fresh orange juice
1 tsp	honey syrup (page 22)
GARNISH	slice of orange, raspberry, mint tip

Combine the ingredients in a shaker with ice and shake. Strain into a wine glass filled with ice. Add the garnish.

Kir

½ oz / 1.5 cl	crème de cassis
5 oz / 15 cl	dry white wine

Pour the crème de cassis into a wine glass. Add the white wine and stir. If you want the drink less sweet, reduce the amount of crème de cassis.

Red Eye

4 oz / 12 cl	red wine
⅔ oz / 2 cl	simple syrup (page 20)
1 oz / 3 cl	fresh lemon juice
1 oz / 3 cl	orange juice
GARNISH	slice of orange

Combine the citrus juices and the simple syrup in a shaker with ice and shake. Strain into a wine glass filled with ice. Add the wine and stir. Slit the orange and place it on the rim of the glass.

Sangria *serves 4*

1 bottle	Spanish red wine
4 oz / 12 cl	Spanish brandy
1 oz / 3 cl	triple sec or Cointreau
2 tsps	superfine (caster) sugar
½ oz / 1.5 cl	fresh lemon juice
½ oz / 1.5 cl	fresh orange juice
GARNISH	half each: apple, orange, lemon, and lime, sliced club soda (optional)

The **Sherry Cobbler**, a twist on the 1860s classic, is a complex cooler to suit any occasion. ❯ ❯ ❯

Pour all ingredients except soda into a pitcher or punch bowl, starting with the sugar. Stir to dissolve sugar. Leave to marinate in the refrigerator for a few hours before serving. When guests arrive, add the slices of lemon, orange, lime, and apple. Add large ice cubes and the club soda. Serve in goblets.

Sherry Cobbler

2 bar spoons	demerara sugar
3 or 4	fresh orange slices
2 oz / 6 cl	medium dry sherry
GARNISH	berries, slice of orange, mint tip

Muddle orange and sugar into a wine glass. Add crushed ice and sherry and stir well until diluted. Top with more crushed ice and the garnish.

Acknowledgments

This book is the result of great teamwork. To my wife, Sue, thanks for your help and unending patience. Thanks to my agent, Fiona Lindsay at Limelight Management, and to everyone who helped out with inspiration for the recipes.

A special thank you to my talented team at Salvatore at Playboy for their help with this rewrite—Stevan Relic, Matteo Belkeziz, Aaron Jones, Arthur Szkoda, Davide Colombo, and Maurizio Palermo.

Photo Credits

The photographer for the original edition of this book was Ian O'Leary, and his photographs also appear in this revised edition. Photographs new to this edition are from the following photographers:

Ian O'Leary: ii, 48 (center), 59 (Applik Delight), 99 (Citrus Touch), 115 (Russian Heart), 165 (Maestro), 173 (Elit Kiss)

Ming Tang-Evans: v, vi, xi (My Martini with a Twist), 25 (Spicy Fifty), 28 (left and right), 37 (My Martini), 45 (Old Fashioned), 48 (right), 62 (Apricot Sour), 67 (Godfrey), 83 (Amalfi Dream), 96 (Breakfast Martini), 112 (Red Earl),

117 (Franklin Cobbler), 118 (Tropical Butterfly), 131 (Grace), 154 (Mayfair Fizz No. 2), 183 (Bunny Bubbles)

Diffords Guide: 35 (Brandy Crusta)

James Duncan: 72 (Singapore Sling)

Nataliya Gorbovskaya: 75 (Cosmopolitan), 85 (Sgroppino al Limone), 107 (El Cerro), 161 (Grasshopper), 176 (Vitamin Hit), 189 (Sherry Cobbler)

Glassware

The following is a list of the glassware that appears in the photographs:

Pages v, 48 (right), 154 (Mayfair Fizz No. 2): Urban Bar art deco coupe

Page vi (Breakfast Martini): Salvatore's Fifty glass

Page 9 (Dirty Martini): Dartington cocktail glass

Page 25 (Spicy Fifty): Urban Bar glass

Page 35 (Brandy Crusta): Salvatore's own late 1800s glass

Page 37 (My Martini): Urban Bar

Page 43 (Level Martini): Baccarat martini glass

Sources

www.dartington.co.uk
www.wildhibiscus.com
www.mariebrizard.com
www.pomwonderful.com

General Index

spicy flavors, 2
spirals, 16–17, 27
spirits. *See also specific
    spirits*
    flavored, 20
    storing, 8
spirits pourer, 4, 5
stir, defined, 27
stirrers, 4
storing spirits and wine, 8
strainer, 4, 5
strawberry flavors, 116–118
strawberry huller, 4
straws, 4
sweet and creamy flavors
    about: overview of, 156
    chocolate, 157–158
    cream, 159–161
    honey, 162–163
sweet flavors, 2
syrups, making, 20–24
    chamomile, 20
    cinnamon, 20
    coconut, 21
    ginger, 21
    gooseberry, 21
    grenadine, 21
    herb-flavored, 22
    honey, 22

mango, 22
passion fruit, 22
pineapple, 23
raspberry, 23
rose, 23
saffron, 23
simple, 20
vanilla, 24

T
tall drink, defined, 27
tea flavors, 138–139
tequila, 31, 40–41
terms, bar, 27
thyme flavors, 140
tomato flavors, 119
tongs, 4, 5
tools, bartender, 4–5
truffle flavors, 169
twists, 18–19, 27

U
unusual flavors, 164–169

V
vanilla flavors, 155
vanilla syrup, 24
vegetable flavors
    about: overview of, 170

asparagus, 171
beet, 172–173
bell pepper, 175
carrot, 177
cucumber, 178
horseradish, 179
rhubarb, 180
zucchini, 181
vermouth flavors, 187
violet flavors, 141
vodka, 42
    flavors, ix–x, 30
    for infusions, 122

W
watermelon flavors, 120–121
wedges, making, 15
whiskey, 44–45
wine
    flavors, 182–189
    glasses, 6, 7
    storing, 8

Z
zest, defined, 27
zester, 4
zucchini flavors, 181

Index by Name

Index by Ingredient

About the Author

Salvatore Calabrese is an international award-winning expert on cocktails and one of the world's most respected bartenders. He is past president of the United Kingdom Bartenders' Guild. He is holder of the Chevalier du Verre Galant and the Chevalier l'Ordre des Côteaux de Champagne, and is Keeper of the Quaiche. His recent awards include 2005: Best New Bar; 2006: Bar of the Year, 2006: Best Cocktail Offering, 2006: Outstanding Achievement Award (Italian Bartenders Association); 2008: Master of the Craft (Australian Bartender Magazine); 2009: Number One (Theme Top 100), 2009: International Cognac Personality of the Year (Bureau National Interprofessionel du Cognac, and Spirits Personality of the Year (Drinking Out Excellence Awards); 2011: Class Awards (Outstanding Achievement to the Industry); 2012: recipient of the World's Best Drink Selection (Spirited Awards at Tales of the Cocktail at New Orleans), 2012: Best Bar 2012 London Lifestyle Awards, and 2012: Guinness World Record, Most Expensive Cocktail. Salvatore Calabrese's illustrious career was also acknowledged in June 2012 by the Italian government with a Gold Medal Award. Additionally, he is a world-renowned authority on Cognac and vintage Cognacs and the author of the worldwide bestsellers *The Complete Home Bartender's Guide* (revised and updated in 2012) and *Classic Cocktails*.

Visit Salvatore Calebrese's website at www.salvatore-calabrese.co.uk and follow him on Twitter @cocktailmaestro.